TREASURES FROM THE NATIONAL MUSEUM BANGKOK

An Introduction
with
157 Color Photographs

THE NATIONAL MUSEUM VOLUNTEERS

Third Reprint : 1995

IN CELEBRATION
OF THE AUSPICIOUS SIXTIETH BIRTHDAY ANNIVERSARY OF
HIS MAJESTY THE KING OF THAILAND
1987

This publication, *Treasures from the National Museum, Bangkok,* represents the results of long term cooperative efforts of many members of the National Museum Volunteers Group. With its numerous illustrations, informative captions and texts, this publication should help to promote, among foreign visitors and residents alike, a wider understanding of the scope and richness of Thai arts as represented in the National Museum collections.

The work of the National Museum Volunteers Group is well known among foreigners in Thailand. Nowadays comprising Thai and foreign members, the Group is dedicated to assisting the Bangkok National Museum in advancing the study and informed appreciation of the Arts of Thailand through a variety of educational and cultural activities.

The Department of Fine Arts is pleased to note that this publication of the National Museum Volunteers Group is offered as a contribution to the celebrations marking the auspicious year of the Sixtieth Birthday of His Majesty the King of Thailand. The proceeds of the sale of this publication will provide funds for current projects of the Group at the National Museum.

Taveesak Senanarong
Director General
Department of Fine Arts.

Over the eighteen years since its foundation, I have been pleased to assist many 'generations' of the National Museum Volunteers Group. During this time, in the course of presenting Guide Training Workshops, Special Lectures and Study Excursions to the group, I have observed that while members are diverse in nationality, professional background and even length of residence in Thailand, they all share a common bond: they are all enthusiastic students of the Arts of Thailand. In this capacity, some of the more recent members of the group have produced this publication as a record of their appreciation and understanding of the many fine examples of the Arts of Thailand as exhibited in the Bangkok National Museum, the 'home base' of the Volunteers Group.

I extend my best wishes for the continuing success of the National Museum Volunteers in the future.

M.C. Subhadradis Diskul
Rector Emeritus
Silpakorn University.

I am pleased to note that the many activities of the National Museum Volunteers are continuing in a productive way. In particular, the regular guided tours, in various languages, presented by the Volunteers provide a valuable service to the general public and overseas tourists visiting the Bangkok National Museum. Similarly, this cooperative publication by the Volunteers should prove to be an attractive souvenir for visitors to the Museum.

Somsak Ratanakul
Director,
Division of National Museums,
Department of Fine Arts.

Since founding the National Museum Volunteers Group over eighteen years ago, I have watched the group grow from its small but enthusiastic beginnings to an organisation that encompasses many cultural and educational activities that are of benefit to its members and the general public, as well as the Bangkok National Museum. Over the years, working closely with the many coordinators and key members of the group, I have been pleased to help the group expand its scope in the promotion of informed understanding of the Arts of Thailand. When, several years ago, members of the group approached me for advice regarding the publication of a souvenir book about fine works of Thai art in the Bangkok National Museum, I was pleased to assist in the arrangements necessary for such an ambitious undertaking. This publication, *Treasures from the National Museum, Bangkok*, is the result: an example of the co-operative efforts and talents of past and present members.

May the National Museum Volunteers Group continue to prosper in their commendable activities.

Chira Chongkol
Former Director,
Division of National Museums,
Department of Fine Arts.

ACKNOWLEDGEMENTS

The National Museum Volunteers Group appreciates the continuing support of the Department of Fine Arts in the many programs undertaken by the Group and extends sincere thanks to the Director-General of the Department of Fine Arts, Khun Taveesak Senanarong.

To our founder, patron and friend, the late Khun Chira Chongkol, former Director of the Division of National Museums, of the Department of Fine Arts, we express our deepest gratitude for guidance and help for many years, and more recently, for facilitating arrangements at the National Museum for this publication.

For advice and comments, particularly in the Sculpture section of the publication, we are indebted to His Serene Highness, Prince Subhadradis Diskul, Rector Emeritus of Silpakorn University, and long-time friend and adviser of the Volunteers Group.

The National Museum Volunteers Group gratefully acknowledges the generous donation from the Foremost Company of Thailand towards printing costs of this publication.

Sincere thanks are also extended to Warner-Lambert (Thailand) Limited, for their donation to this project.

In addition, the John F. Kennedy Foundation is sincerely thanked for long term support and encouragement of this endeavour.

Many thanks are also due to the Kodak Company of Thailand for their assistance.

The production of the publication has been a long term group effort of the National Museum Volunteers. Many members, both past and present, have given of their time and talents through various Volunteer activities to make this possible. Their skills and leadership are gratefully acknowledged.

Special thanks are due to Martine Dean, from whose original concept, inspiration and guidance the book first took shape, to Virginia M. Di Crocco who, as Coordinator of the National Museum Volunteers at that time, initiated the project, and to Rita Ringis who, as Coordinating Editor, took over the task of bringing this project to its conclusion. National Museum Volunteers photographer Pam Taylor and National Museum Staff photographer Khun Somchai Vorasastra are most appreciatively acknowledged for their excellence, expertise and long term commitment to the project. Many thanks go also to Helene Sackstein, Layout Editor.

However, none of this would have been possible without the cooperation and continuing support of the National Museum. To Khun Somsak Ratanakul, Director of the Division of National Museums, Department of Fine Arts, to Khun Khamthornthep Kraithaithong, Head of Curatorial Staff Section, to Khun Somlak Charoenpot, Head of the National Museum, Bangkok, and to the staff of the National Museum, the Volunteers offer their sincere thanks.

National Museum Volunteers Group
Bangkok 1987

CONTENTS

Prehistory

Ban Chiang is a busy village built atop a long mound rising above the ricefields near Udon Thani on Thailand's Northeast Plateau. Although superficially akin to thousands of similar settlements, Ban Chiang is now famous for two distinctive features. It is the type site of a handsome family of prehistoric earthenware pottery which exerts a unique aesthetic attraction. In addition, it has given its name to a flourishing bronze- and iron-age culture that because of its early technical accomplishments has caused the rethinking of long-held opinions regarding when and where some basic skills of civilization may have developed.

Traditionally, prehistoric Southeast Asia had been considered as culturally stagnant and passive, merely the recipient of innovation from China and India. Only a handful of original thinkers felt that Southeast Asia could well be the site of the domestication of food plants, which would give rise to other technical advances. Their ideas were confirmed in the 1960 s when archaeological fieldwork in Northwest Thailand turned up evidence of the intensive use of plants, perhaps indicating their domestication, as early as 9700 B.C., as well as pottery dated to 6800 B.C., dates whose surprising antiquity gave a jolt to concepts of the primacy of the Middle East in such matters. At about the same time, excavations in Northeast Thailand unearthed skillfully crafted bronze artifacts, fine sandstone molds for metal production in quantity, and the world's oldest socketed tool, datable to as early as 2300–3600 B.C.

Then, in 1974 and 1975, an international team confirmed the existence at Ban Chiang of a well-developed, extensive and long enduring bronze and iron culture that no one had ever known about before. Moreover, Ban Chiang's 'lost bronze age' rivalled and perhaps exceeded in antiquity other bronze ages from

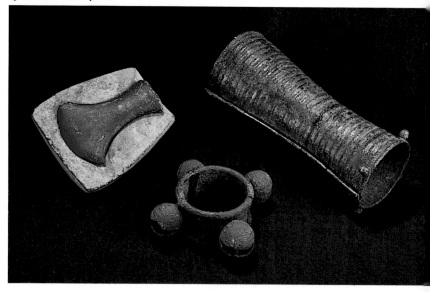

1

Ban Chiang culture bronze artifacts. Socketed tool, set in sandstone mold. 10 cm long. Bracelet. 20 cm long. Bangle, with bells. 8 cm diameter.

better-known parts of the world.

The implications of the discoveries at Ban Chiang and elsewhere in Thailand are manifold. Eyes must turn now to Southeast Asia for information of major importance regarding mankind's earliest efforts at developing skills fundamental to technical progress. Furthermore, the incidence on mainland Southeast Asia of a cultural center as advanced as Ban Chiang, dating back to perhaps six thousand years ago, when evaluated with bold new linguistic hypotheses, raises the unprecedented but serious suggestions that the flow of cultural innovation may have been northward to China from a center in what is now Thailand, rather than in the other direction; that the vast trans-Pacific migration of the Austronesians may have been given impetus from just such a center; and, as some Thai scholars have ventured to propose, that perhaps the Thais have been living here in Thailand for longer than anyone has previously dared to guess. ■

2 Rooster, and chicken coop. Bronze. 7 cm high. Late Metal Age. Found at Don Tha Phet. The bronze coop is very similar to woven bamboo coops used in Thai villages today.

3 Peacock. Bronze. 8 cm high. Late Metal Age. Found at Don Tha Phet.

The discovery and study of prehistoric cultures in Thailand is a relatively recent phenomenon. Until the middle of this century, such discoveries were largely accidental. Since the 1960 s, systematic and ongoing archaeological investigations on prehistoric sites have revealed that complex cultures flourished in the region. Sites include Spirit Cave in northern Thailand, Non Nok Tha and Ban Chiang in the northeast, Ban Kao and Don Tha Phet in the Kanchanaburi region. Perhaps the most famous and most controversial at present is the site of Ban Chiang.

The Bangkok National Museum collection includes fine ceramics (see p. 56) and bronzes that provide tantalising glimpses into the lives and technologies of these prehistoric peoples.

Sculpture

The early sculptors of Thailand were faced with an awe-inspiring task. For it was their responsibility to capture the intangible, invisible gods and translate their power, their beauty and their spirituality into figures of stone or bronze. Fortunately a number of guidelines existed to help them. Since most of the early images carved in the region were representations of either Hindu deities or the Buddha, the sculptors were obliged to follow certain rules, originally devised in India, the source of both religions.

It was most important, for instance, that an image of the Buddha should not be confused with any ordinary person, or indeed with a Hindu deity. In India, the very earliest images of the Buddha were not made until several hundred years after his death, and since no realistic portrait of him existed, the Buddhist authorities invented thirty-two special features which were to be included in a true and instantly recognizable image of the Buddha.

In practice it was not possible to include every feature in each image, but the most important ones are always present. For instance, Buddha images display a strange, unnatural lump on the top of the head. This is called the *ushnisa*. It is symbolic of the Buddha's wisdom and is one of the key identifying features.

The body and limbs of a Buddha image are depicted in a highly stylised fashion and show little evidence of bone or muscle. This in no way reflects the inability of the early sculptors to model the human physique more accurately. It is the result of the way that several of the thirty-two special features were combined in an endeavour to portray the Buddha's superiority to the average man, and his profound spiritual purity. In Thailand his body is asexual, this aspect signifying the conquering of

physical desire by the disciplining of his mind. The Buddha's eyes are usually downcast, shaped like the buds of lotus flowers, and the mouth smiles gently to enhance the aura of inner peace.

Thailand's early sculptors had the advantage of being able to copy images brought here by visitors from India where a perfection of style had been reached by about the 5th century AD. It was not the sculptors'job to be innovative; the more perfectly they copied a beautiful image, the better it was considered to be. However, it was only natural that local craftsmen should begin to breathe new life into old forms, and with the passage of years local features and preferences of style became more and more evident. Indeed, after many centuries, the styles can be seen to have changed quite dramatically. The astonishing thing is that so many craftsmen, never exposed to sophisticated schools of art or theoretical concepts, managed so successfully to create images of outstanding beauty and individuality, which without doubt portray the serenity and the spirituality of the Buddha nature.

The versatility of the indigenous sculptors can be seen in the way they also handled the crafting of Hindu images, which were conceived in quite a different manner to images of the Buddha. The three

major Hindu gods, Brahma, Vishnu, and Siva, were super-humans. Frequently possessing four or more arms, their images radiate power. Their broad, muscular chests and proud stance epitomise masculine vigour. Their faces portray inner strength and beauty. Not surprisingly, the consorts of these gods tend to be the embodiment of seductive feminine grace and sweetness.

Hindu gods are distinguished from each other by various attributes assigned to them which are associated with their legendary origins. Brahma is the only one usually presented with four faces. Frequently they are accorded kingly status, being crowned and adorned with jewels, and providing the sculptors with a wonderful opportunity to reveal their skill at intricate, delicate and detailed carving, as well as a mastery of mass and proportion.

And yet we know very little about the early sculptors themselves. We do not know the name of a single one of them. Just occasionally the name of a patron or donor will appear in an inscription, but the name of the sculptor is never revealed. We are indeed fortunate that such a wealth of their work survives, a marvelous testimony to their devotion and skill. ∎

4 ————————————————————————————
Bodhi Tree. Stone. 45 cm high. Found at Ayutthaya. Carved in high relief, this tree with its characteristic heart–shaped leaves represents the sacred tree under which Gautama meditated and achieved Enlightenment, becoming henceforth known as the Buddha.

In the Bangkok National Museum, fine sculptures of religious significance are displayed according to a general chronological order. Each period of sculpture, though sometimes overlapping with other periods in time, is denoted by a title that incorporates either the name of a dominant kingdom or major characteristic of the time. The following pages, through text and pictures, celebrate the great and varied traditions of sculptural expression of religious ideals in Thailand, traditions that span some fifteen hundred years until the early 20th century.

Mon Dvaravati Sculpture

The collapse of the Funan Empire in the mid-sixth century A.D. permitted the emergence of many independent states throughout Southeast Asia. In Thailand one of these states was called Dvaravati and its centre appears to have been at the head of the Bight of Bangkok, off the Gulf of Thailand. The main cities were Nakhon Pathom, Lopburi and U Thong. The word 'Dvaravati' is also used to describe an art style that flourished from the 7th-11th century A.D. throughout almost the entire area of present-day Thailand.

Important sites of Dvaravati architectural remains and art objects include Nakhon Pathom, U Thong and Khu Bua in the central area, Dong Si Maha Phot to the east and Muang Fa Daed in the northeast. To the south Dvaravati culture penetrated as far as Songkhla. The most northerly site of Dvaravati influence was Haripunjaya (modern Lamphun) which persisted until the late 13th century A.D.

Little is known about the political organization of Dvaravati. It was most probably a kingdom which consisted of a group of cities loosely linked together by cultural and family ties. What we do know of Dvaravati derives mainly from the vast amount of superb sculpture which remains.

The majority of the people of Dvaravati were Mon and the language they spoke was Mon, which is related to the Khmer language and to several other dialects still spoken throughout Southeast Asia. Judging from the predominant finds, the religion of the Mon was Hinayana Buddhism. During the mid-Dvaravati period – 8th – 9th century

5

Wheel of the Law, and Deer, Lime-Stone. 95 cm diameter. 7–8th century, Dvaravati. Found at Nakhon Pathom.

A considerable number of Wheels of the Law have been found in the Nakhon Pathom and western region. These wheels, often found together with reclining deer, are symbolic of the ever expanding, ever-turning Buddhist doctrine, set in motion by the first sermon the Buddha preached in the Deer Park in Sarnath, India. The votive tablet (fig.6 above) suggests that the wheels may have been placed on tall columns.

Wheels of the Law are carved on both sides with floral motifs derived from the Gupta and post-Gupta styles of India. This wheel has two important features: its spokes are carved completely in the round, and it bears on one side a Pali inscription of the Four Noble Truths of Buddhism.

6

Votive tablet. Stone. 10 cm high. 8–10th Century, Dvaravati. Found at Khu Bua, Ratchaburi.

The Buddha is seated in the attitude of meditation with the legs loosely crossed. He is protected by a parasol, and flanked by the Wheel of the Law raised high on a column on his right, and a Dvaravati type stupa on his left.

A.D.–Mahayana Buddhism was also practised. Some finds of sculptures of Hindu gods indicate that Hinduism was followed too.

The Mon were highly skilled artists who excelled in stone sculpture, stucco and terra cotta architectural decoration, and, to a lesser degree, in bronze work. Their art style was mainly influenced by the Gupta and post-Gupta styles which flourished in central and western India between the 4th and 8th centuries. However, the facial features of Dvaravati Buddha images exhibit pronounced native elements—a large face, curved eyebrows joined at the bridge of the nose, prominent eyes partly closed, a broad nose, thick and well-defined lips. The hair is in large spiral curls with a cylindrical ushnisha or cranial protuberance. In contrast to earlier Gupta influenced images which display a *tribhanga* or triple flexion curve of the body, later standing Dvaravati im-

ages exhibit rigid symmetry: the body stands in erect posture with the feet firmly planted on a lotus pedestal; both hands perform the same mudra; the outer robe covers both shoulders and clings closely to the body, giving an impression of nude asexuality; both sides of the robe are identical. Seated Buddha images are either in Indian style (with legs crossed or folded), or in 'European' style (with legs hanging down).

A distinctive contribution of Dvaravati sculpture is the large free-standing Wheel of the Law, an aniconic symbol of the Buddha's First Sermon. Although they are found in India as well, where they symbolized the Chakravartin, or Universal Emperor, their occurrence in Southeast Asia is limited to Dvaravati areas. Decorated with floral patterns which show Gupta influence, these wheels were erected on high pillars and placed in temple compounds. ■

7

Buddha image (detail of full length statue). Limestone. 145 cm high. 7–8th century, Dvaravati. Found at Wat Na Phra Men, Ayutthaya.

The serene face of this limestone Buddha image still shows traces of lacquer. The features are typical of Dvaravati images: conical ushnisha, large hair curls, eyebrows joined at the bridge of the nose, three-quarters closed eyes elongated toward the temples, high cheek-bones, prominent nose and full lips raised at the corners.

8

Standing Buddha image. Limestone. 147 cm high. Early 8th century, Dvaravati. Found at Wat Raw, Ayutthaya.

This limestone standing Buddha image resembles Indian Gupta prototypes: the body is slightly flexed; the transparent robe covering both shoulders clings closely to the body; the face is soft and gentle but incorporates Mon features; the right hand performs the gesture of blessing, while the left hand, originally separately pegged but now missing, held the robe.

9

Head of an image of Buddha, Terracotta. 20 cm high. 7–8th century, Dvaravati. Found at Wat Phra Ngam, Nakhon Pathom.

Evoking feelings no words can convey, this delicate red clay head of the Buddha was found at Nakhon Pathom together with other pieces in terracotta and stucco, and was probably part of the decoration of a stupa.

10

Heads of divinities and demon guardian. Stucco. Heights from top of page: 15 cm, 25 cm, 30 cm. 8–10th century. Dvaravati.

These bas relief stucco pieces were found at Nakhon Pathom and were probably originally used as architectural decorations. The heads of divinities, display typical Mon features, similar to those seen on Buddha images of the time.

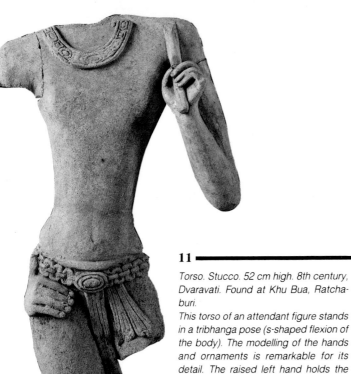

11

Torso. Stucco. 52 cm high. 8th century, Dvaravati. Found at Khu Bua, Ratchaburi.

This torso of an attendant figure stands in a tribhanga pose (s-shaped flexion of the body). The modelling of the hands and ornaments is remarkable for its detail. The raised left hand holds the handle of a fly-whisk in the gracefully curved fingers while the right hand rests on the slender hip.

13

Bodhisattva. Terracotta. 91 cm high. 8th century. Dvaravati. Found at Khu Bua. Ratchaburi.

Such youthful and graceful figures represent Mahayana Bodhisattvas, saintly beings who have attained Enlightenment but have postponed Parinirvana until they have helped all mankind to reach the goal of release from suffering and endless rebirths.

Found at Khu Bua, this striking figure is regarded as one of the finest Dvaravati works in terracotta. The hairstyle, broad shoulders, slender body, and the tribhanga pose are reminiscent of Indian Gupta and post–Gupta art. The figure is probably the Bodhisattva Avalokitesvara as indicated by the antelope skin worn diagonally across the torso.

12

Head of an image of a Bodhisattva. Terracotta, 38 cm high. 7th century, Dvaravati. Found at Khu Bua, Ratchaburi.

18

14

Standing Buddha image. Bronze. 49 cm high. 8–9th century, Dvaravati, Found at Wat Choeng Tha, Nonthaburi. With the outer robe covering both shoulders, and the hands symmetrically aligned performing the gesture of preaching, this image reflects the regard for symmetry which was to prevail in later Dvaravati images. This gesture executed with both hands by a standing Buddha image is generally regarded in Thailand as signifying the Buddha's Descent from Tavatimsa Heaven, where he had preached to his mother.

15

Standing Buddha image. Bronze. 110 cm high. 8–9th century, Dvaravati. Found at Muang Fai, Buriram.
Discovered by chance by a villager in 1972, this standing image is the largest Dvaravati bronze image found in Thailand. Rigidly symmetrical in attire and gesture, this image performs the preaching mudra.

Ancient Hindu Gods

Because of its geographical position midway in the Southeast Asian region, ancient Thailand served as a gateway for Indian trade with Cambodia and regions further north as early as the third to fifth centuries A.D.

That certain widely dispersed areas developed as prosperous Indian trade entrepots is evident in the discovery of particularly fine Indian-influenced sculptures dating from the 6th to 9th centuries A.D. in the Southern Peninsular regions of Thailand, such as at Takua Pa (Phang Nga Province), and at Chaiya (Surat Thani Province), as well as deep within the interior, at Dong Si Maha Phot (Prachinburi Province) and at Si Thep (Petchabun Province).

Sculptural representations and emblems of various Hindu gods have been found. These include the god Shiva, usually represented by the linga or phallic symbol, the earlier dated ones being carved in a realistic manner whereas the later ones are more stylized, and may have the face of the god carved on them (ekamukhalinga).

In archaeological findings, the images of Vishnu, or his avatar Krishna, predominate. These beautiful images are imbued with a dynamic masculine grace and differ profoundly from the traditionally serene and static images of the Buddha.

Images of the multiple armed Vishnu found in the South were carved either in high relief against a back support slab or in the full round. In the latter case, support was provided by the legs and robe flap at the base, and perhaps by the club that the statue held, as suggested by vestiges of it still visible on the base.

Images of Vishnu or his avatar, Krishna, found (at Si Thep) in north central Thailand, differ from those of the Peninsula in aesthetic vitality as well as apparently technical innovation in their modelling, as the former appear to have been carved fully in the round, without any supporting structures. In contrast to the Peninsular images, these Si Thep images display the god clothed in the barest of coverings, usually only the suggestion of a loincloth draped between the legs. The austere simplicity of the sculptures contrasts with the intricately curled coiffure of the images.

17

Vishnu. Stone, 202 cm high. 6–7th century, Peninsular Art. Found at Phra Narai Hill, Takua Pa, Phang Nga Province, 1929.
This image with its powerful muscular torso and limbs symbolises the might of Vishnu, the Preserver of the Universe. At the base is the vestige of a club the image once held, originally providing added support for this monumental image executed daringly in the full round.

While the Peninsular images are generally symmetrical in stance and gesture, the Si Thep images have a daring and graceful asymmetry of posture, with the body in the sinuous or s-shaped curve, the disposition of the arms further enhancing this asymmetry. Presumably because these images were carved without supports, only torsos with partially intact arms and legs survive. Even so, their grace and vitality are undeniable. ∎

16

Ekamukhalinga. Stone. 109 cm high. 6th century, Peninsular Art. Found at Chaiya, Surat Thani.
This phallic representation of Shiva derives undoubtedly from an Indian prototype and displays the stern face of the god.

Krishna. Stone. 104 cm high. 6–8th century. Found at Si Thep, Petchabun. Though badly damaged, this image with its ornate coiffure, broad shoulders and slim curved body is undoubtedly one of the masterpieces in the National Museum. The graceful posture represents Krishna holding aloft the mountain to protect his followers from a wrathful flood.

18

Vishnu or Krishna. Stone. 119 cm high. 7–8th century. Found at Si Thep, Petchabun.
The high headdress suggests this image, in graceful tribhanga pose, is Vishnu. However, the position of the upraised arm may indicate this is Krishna, Avatar of Vishnu, upholding the mountain Govardhana to protect his devotees.

19

Vishnu Stone. 148 cm high. 7–8th century. Peninsular Art. Found at Wieng Sa, Surat Thani.
Austere and virile, this image may originally have been decorated with removable ornaments. Although the posterior arms are broken off, traces of the god's emblems are visible in the remaining hands. The pedestal retains vestiges of the club and sash.

Srivijaya and Peninsular Sculpture

According to inscriptions, a powerful empire known as Srivijaya, ruled by the Sailendra dynasty from Central Java, held sway in the Indonesian archipelago and the Malay peninsula from the late 7th to the end of the 13th century A.D. By the end of the last quarter of the 8th century, this Srivijaya empire appears to have expanded its power into peninsular Thailand as far as the Isthmus of Kra, possibly to ensure the establishment of safe land routes for commerce between India and China, avoiding the Straits of Malacca, where piracy prevailed between the 6th and the 8th centuries.

The location of the Srivijaya capital itself is the object of much ongoing debate. Some scholars believe that it was based in Palembang in South Sumatra, where five stone inscriptions dated to the last quarter of the 7th century A.D. have been found. Others believe it may have been located in Southern Thailand, at Chaiya, where many antiquities have been unearthed, but so far only one stone inscription dated 775 A.D. has been discovered there. This inscription records the construction of Mahayana Buddhist monuments by the kings of Srivijaya, and mentions a dynastic marriage between the royal house of Chaiya (Southern Thailand) and the Sailendra or ruling dynasty of Central Java, thus cementing close relations between the two countries in the last quarter of the 8th century A.D. This Sailendra dynasty practised Mahayana Buddhism. Sculptural and architectural relics dating from the 8th to 13th centuries found in Southern Thailand reveal that Mahayana Buddhism also predominated in the Peninsular region during that time. The art of this period and region is known as Srivijaya after the name of this extended maritime kingdom. Its sculptures are varied and the date attributed to each of them is tentative. Several artistic influences have contributed to this style. Before the 8th century A.D. a distinctive Mon influence, coming from the Mon kingdom of Dvaravati in Central

21

Bodhisattva. Bronze, with silver inlay. 63 cm high. 8–9th century. Srivijaya. Found at Chaiya, Surat Thani by H.R.H. Prince Damrong Rajanubhab in 1905. This image is thought to be Padmapani, a form of Avalokitesvara. It is clear that the image was carved fully in the round and stood in the tribangha pose. The scarf underneath the sacred cord depicts an antelope head, indicative of Avalokitesvara.

22

22

*Bodhisattva Avalokitesvara. Stone. 114
cm high. 6–7th century. Srivijaya.
Found at Chaiya, Surat Thani.*

This image of Avalokitesvara is one of
the earliest and most beautiful stone
sculptures found in Peninsular Thailand. Modelled on the Indian Gupta and
post-Gupta school, he has retained the
tribangha pose or triple flexion of the
body, the right hip thrust out, the left
knee bent. He wears a long dhoti se-
cured by a narrow belt. A figure of the
Buddha Amitabha in the lower part of
the chignon, and the antelope skin
hanging from the left shoulder, identify
the figure as Avalokitesvara.

23

*Bodhisattva Avalokitesvara. Bronze. 72
cm high. 9–10th century, Srivijaya.
Found at Wat Phra Boromthat, Chaiya,
Surat Thani.*

This Avalokitesvara is highly decorated with ornate jewelry showing the
influence of the Indo-Javanese school
of bronze sculpture. The eight arms and
legs are broken but the headdress is
complete, showing a small figure of the
Buddha, Amitabha, indicative of Avalokitesvara.

Thailand, is evident in early Srivijaya art. However, in the main, the art of Srivijaya bears close resemblance to Indo-Javanese art, reflecting complex influences from India: Amaravati, Gupta and Pala. From the 11th century, when most of central and northeastern Thailand came under Khmer suzerainty, Khmer influence is also discernible in late Srivijaya sculptures.

Towards the middle of the 13th century A.D. the Srivijaya empire began to break apart, possibly because of the consolidation of Chinese maritime supremacy at the end of the Sung dynasty (960–1279 A.D.). In addition, as recorded in King Ramkhamhaeng's stone inscription of 1292 A.D., the powerful new kingdom of Sukhothai in the north penetrated the peninsula as far as Nakhon Sri Thammarat, bringing the southern regions under its rule.

24 ▪ 25 ▪ 26

Votive Tablets. Clay. 8–9th century. Srivijaya. Discovered in caves in Peninsular Thailand.

Bodhi leaf shaped votive tablet. 6.5 cm diameter. A four armed Bodhisattva, Padmapani seated on a lotus, is flanked by an inscription in an Indian script extolling the Buddhist teachings.

Votive tablet. Clay, 9.5 cm high. This depicts the Dhyani Buddha Amitabha, seated in meditation under an umbrella in the Western Paradise, bestowing immortality on departed souls that go there. He is flanked by Bodhisattvas and a small stupa.

Votive tablet. Clay 6.5 cm diameter. A Buddha is seated in the center, flanked by two attendants. Of interest here is the depiction of structures reminiscent of Javanese architecture, below which appears an inscription.

Buddhist texts relate that during a storm, Muchalinda, the Naga or Serpent King gave shelter to the meditating Buddha by encircling his body with its coils and spreading its multi-headed hood over the Buddha's head as protection. Generally, in sculpture in Thailand, this event is depicted with the Buddha seated on the coils of the Naga.

27▪28

Buddha under Naga. Bronze. 165 cm high. 1291 A.D. From Wat Wieng. Chaiya. Surat Thani.

This large bronze image is often called the Buddha of Grahi, the ancient name for the present site of Chaiya. This is an interesting statue as the Buddha, seated in a folded leg posture on the coils of Naga, is in the position of Subduing Mara, and not in meditation as is usual when he is portrayed with the Naga. There is a five-line inscription in the Khmer language on the pedestal and a date now interpreted as equivalent to A.D. 1291. The Naga shows strong Khmer features, particularly in the style of the Naga heads, while the plain cranial protuberance on the head of the Buddha, decorated with a bodhi leaf, and the wide pleated end of the robe on the left shoulder, denote late Srivijayan development, seen in Peninsular Thailand in the 13th and 14th centuries.

Khmer and Lopburi Sculpture

In about the 6th century A.D. the Khmer, a people linguistically related to the Mon, came down the Mekhong River valley. Some settled in Northeastern Thailand; others went on to the area which is now Cambodia. By the following century statues bearing the impact of Khmer style were being sculpted in what is now Thailand. From the 7th century to the mid 13th, the military prowess of the Khmer increased until a large portion of Thailand was under their control; finally in the 13th century the Thais were able to rise up, overcome the Khmer and become their own masters.

The art of the Khmer in Thailand has often been called Lopburi Art after the city of that name in Central Thailand which was the major Khmer seat of provincial administration. This designation has been given to indicate that the art is not merely the creation of the Khmer from the Angkor area but that of the local peoples as well, who introduced new stylistic ideas of their own and left their distinctive imprint.

The sculpture of the Khmer was meant to be viewed in the round. The bodies of the early images are especially well articulated. The anatomy is presented correctly, carefully, sensitively and naturally. This is the case with the 8th–9th century bronze four-armed Bodhisattva in plate 30, one of the many Mahayanist deities from Prakhon Chai on the Korat Plateau in Northeastern Thailand. Not only is the youthful body finely delineated but the face and headdress show a master's hand. Of the same period is the magnificent bronze head of yet another Mahayanist deity, thought to be Maitreya, the future Buddha, although the stupa which probably once adorned the elaborate headdress to indicate Maitreya (plate 31) is now missing. The 70 cm height of the head gives an indication of the tremendous size of the bronze image and at the same-time of the technical as well as artistic capabilites of the creators.

29

Guardian lion. Stone. 157 cm high. 12–13th century, Lopburi, Khmer Bayon style. Lions were considered guardians of the Buddhist teachings, and their images were placed at temple doorways.

Much of the Khmer sculpture is of stone. An outstanding example is the figure of Uma, the wife of the Hindu god Shiva (plate 39). She is presented as a youthful figure with braided hair and firm breasts. The upper part of her body is left uncovered as is usually the case with statues of Khmer feminine figures. She wears a long pleated sarong with a U-shaped top at the front, typical of the style of the 11th century, often called the Baphuon after the type site in Cambodia. The lissome dancing feminine figures in plate 38 are probably a half century or so later. So is the extremely finely wrought statue of a Vajrayana or Tantric Buddhist deity seen dancing with one leg poised high in dramatic action (plate 37). Vajrayana Buddhism often called Tantrism, had come to Thailand from India via Cambodia by the 10th century and had made significant inroads in the art of Northeastern Thailand by late Baphuon and early Angkor Wat (1110–1175 A.D.) times. The style of the period is indicated by the male Somphot or loin cloth with the U at the front and a butterfly bow at the back. The figure wears a diadem and has a conical headdress

The Buddha image during the Baphuon and following periods was often depicted seated upon the coils of the great naga Muchalinda, with seven hooded heads of the serpent providing protection above. Unlike Mon art, where the heads are outward-looking, the subordinate heads of the Khmer-influenced nagas look upward towards the central head. Crowned Buddha images were popular: an excellent example is the Angkor Wat period crowned Buddha protected by the Naga, found at Wat Na Phra Men in Ayutthaya (plate 32). This regal-looking figure of stone wears long ear pendants and has a conical ushnisha decorated with lotus petals.

The standing crowned Buddha image also of the Angkor Wat pe-riod in plate 33 has been decorated with many of the ornaments of royalty. He wears not only a crown and long ear pendants but armlets and an elaborate necklace and belt as well; in affixing such decorations the sculptor was reinforcing the concept of the Buddha as a universal emperor. It is thought that initially the Khmer decorated the images with real jewelry but as time went by the sculptors placed the adornments directly on the images. The Buddha has both hands in the *abhaya mudra* or gesture of Dispelling Fear.

Hindu deities also were of tremendous importance in Lopburi Art as is indicated by the crowned Angkor Wat period image of the Hindu God Vishnu dominating a lintel that once capped a doorway of a Khmer temple. During the Angkor Wat period, scenes depicting stories were very popular decoration for lintels. On the lintel in plate 40, the Hindu god Vishnu sleeps on an aquatic animal floating on the primeval waters. The universe has been destroyed and he is dreaming an ideal vision of what the new universe should be. From his navel rises a radiant lotus and from this lotus emerges Brahma, the creator, at the center, with a deity on each side. At the feet of Vishnu are his two consorts, Bhumi, the goddess of the Earth, and Lakshmi, the goddess of Fortune.

The Angkor Wat Period was followed by the Bayon, named after the huge Buddhist complex at Angkor Thom built by the great Khmer king, Jayavarman VII (1181–1219 A.D.). The sculpture of a man (plate 36) found at Phimai, the most important Khmer temple in the Northeastern part of Thailand, is thought to be the portrait of King Jayavarman VII. That remarkable ruler was about 55 to 60 years of age when he attained the throne.

He had become a firm adherent of an obscure Tantric cult worshipping a trinity consisting of

30

Bodhisattva. Bronze. 141 cm high. 8–9th century, Khmer Kompong Prae style. Found at Prakhjon| Chai.

In Mahayana Buddhism, images of Bodhisattvas represent saint-like beings to whom devotees may pray.

the Buddha, the Bodhisattva Avalokitesvara and the feminine deity, Prajnaparamita, the goddess of transcendental wisdom. The facial expression of the image is that of a person who has reached complete contentment and peace. The smile is sweet and introspective and the eyes are downcast as if in deep thought. After a turbulent life, the king, it would seem, had realized eternal bliss and was anxious to share his discoveries with others. Soon this smile appeared on images throughout the realm. One of the most significant of these is that of the radiating Avalokitesvara (plate 35) who represents compassion and is an emanation of the Buddha Amitabha of the Western Paradise. The figure of the Buddha Amitabha is in the headdress. The upper part of the Bodhisattva's body is entirely covered with tiny images. More images adorn the ankles and toes like bands of anklets and toe-rings. At the center of the chest and in the region around the waist are seated crowned figures, apparently female and probably representing Prajnaparamita. Again the face has a sweet introspective smile as the image radiates hope and protection in every direction. Little thought has been given to the body itself. The spiritual projection is much more important than any physical considerations.

In the art of the period animals and birds are often depicted since they play meaningful roles in popular beliefs. The Garuda is a huge bird with broad wings, capable of high flight and full of courage; as such he represents the sun. His eternal enemy is the naga, who lives in the oceans and thus indicates the waters. Together they suggest fertility. The bronze Garuda in plate 41 was used as a fitting of a chariot.

The Buddha has often been described in leonine terms since the lion is the most powerful and noblest of the beasts. Lions were often used to adorn Khmer tem-

31

Bodhisattva, Head from a colossal image. Bronze. 70 cm high. 8th century, Khmer Kompong Prae style. Found in Nakhon Ratchasima Province.
The intricate headdress of this Bodhisattva may originally have featured a model of a stupa, which would identify the image as Maitreya or the Buddha of the Future in Mahayanist beliefs.

ples. Those of the Bayon period, like the stone lion in plate 29 are distinguished by their V-shaped vests simulating chain mail and their very toothy, broadly smiling mouths.

After the death of King Jayavarman VII the Khmer began to lose their hold both militarily and artistically. The design of the post-Bayon Buddha image (Plate 42) perhaps presages the imminent freedom of the Thais. The facial expression is still very gentle but the eyes are open and very much aware of the surroundings. The long shoulder flap and line of the robe over the arm suggest a renewed influence from Pala India via Cambodia. The ear lobes are long as if they once had jeweled earrings dangling from them. The ushnisha is formed of lotus petals. Most significantly, there is a broad band on the forehead, a feature that would become synonymous with the forthcoming U Thong art and the early art of the Thai kingdom of Ayutthaya. ∎

32

Crowned Buddha image on Naga. Stone. 1.8 m high. 12th century, Khmer Angkor Wat style. Found at Wat Na Phra Men at Ayutthaya, 1929. Austere and regal, this image represents the Buddha as universal ruler. Interestingly, the upper part of the body is sculpted as if bare, with the lower part of the robe being indicated at the waist and ankles.

33

Crowned Standing Buddha image. Bronze. 55 cm high. 12-13th century, Lopburi style.
Dressed in royal attire, this image performs the gesture of Dispelling Fear Palms of the hands are decorated with the Wheel of the Law.

34

Ceremonial utensil with Vajrasattva. Bronze. 42.3 cm high. 11-13th century, Lopburi style.
This utensil may be a candle holder used in circumambulatory rituals. The central figure, Vajrasattva, a Buddha worshipped by the Mahayanist Vajrayana sect, holds his attributes of a double thunderbolt and bell.

35

Radiating Avalokitesvara. Stone. 155 cm high. 13th century, Khmer Bayon style. Found at Prasat Muang Singh, on the Kwæ Noi River at Kanchanaburi.

Dressed in Bayon style, and adorned on torso and arms with many tiny images, this originally eight armed figure represents the All Compassionate One, Bodhisattva Avalokitesvara, who looks down upon the earth with mercy for all mankind. Indicative of Avalokitesvara is the seated Buddha Amitabha in the headdress.

36

King Jayavarman VII. Stone. 1.42 m high. Late 12th-early 13th century, Khmer Bayon style. Found at Phimai Sanctuary, Nakhon Ratchasima Province.

Though seated in a position similar to that of Buddha images, this vigorous and masculine sculpture is a portrait of a king, rare in Buddhist art.

Now in the National Museum Phimai

37

Deity. Bronze. 12.5 cm high. 13th century, Lopburi style.

This Tantric Buddhist deity dances to stamp out ignorance in the Universe.

38 ━━━━━━━━━━━━━

*Fragment with Dancing Apsaras.
Bronze. 11 cm high. 12th century
(?) Found in Kalasin Province.*

*Apsaras or celestial maidens are
the heavenly companions of heroes
who have fallen in battle.*

39 ━━━━━━━━━━━━━

*Uma. Stone. 60 cm high. 11th century,
Khmer Baphuon style.*

*Consort of the Hindu god Shiva, this
beautiful stone figure provides us
with a glimpse of feminine fashions
of the time.*

40

Lintel. Stone. 179 cm long, 62 cm high. 12-13th century, Khmer Baphuon style.

Lintels ornamented doorways to Khmer temples. The scene depicted on this lintel symbolises the re- creation of the universe after it has suffered a cyclic destruction. Reclining on an aquatic creature, the god Vishnu dreams the ideal universe. Flanked by two flying celestial beings, and seated on a lotus which emanates from Vishnu's navel, is the four faced god Brahma, the Creator, whose task it is to put the dream into effect.

41

Garuda. Bronze. 49.5 cm high. 13-14th century, Lopburi style.

This magnificent chariot fitting represents the half-man, half-bird, Garuda, the mount of the Hindu god Vishnu.

42

*Detail of seated Buddha image.
Sandstone. 100 cm high. 13-14th
century, Lopburi style.*
*This image has a serenely smiling
expression typical of the Khmer Bayon
period. Separating the hairline and
forehead is a broad band, and the
ushnisha or cranial protuberance, is
ornamented by lotus petals, characteristic of Thai Lopburi art.*

Lan Na Thai Sculpture

A theory that traditionally has been given considerable credence holds that by the 11th century A.D., migrating Thai tribes had infiltrated and settled in regions of northern Thailand. By 1297, under the leadership of the dynamic King Mangrai, a northern kingdom known as Lan Na Thai extended from Chiang Saen in the far north through to Chiang Rai, Chiang Mai, Lamphun and Lampang. Chiang Mai was established as the capital of the kingdom, which shared the Buddhist beliefs and to some extent the culture of the earlier Mon kingdom of Haripunjaya in the Lamphun region.

The art produced in the Lan Na Thai Kingdom between 11th and 18th centuries A.D. is the object of current scholarly debate, as many influences have contributed to its distinctive qualities, including those from Haripunjaya. Angkor, Sukhothai, Sri Lanka, India and Burma. Though there is much controversy over the origin and dating of northern Buddha images, this Lan Na region can be said to have produced two distinctive types. The first type is sometimes called Early Chiang Saen after the town where many such images were found, whereas the second type has traditionally been known as Late Chiang Saen or Chiang Mai.

43 ────────

Seated Buddha image. Bronze, 73 cm high. Early Chiang Saen style. Lan Na.

The Buddha. seated on a lotus pedestal in the vajrasana or crossed-leg posture, performs the mudra Victory over Mara, signifying the moment of Enlightenment. Also characteristic of early Chiang Saen style, the oval face is plump, with a pronounced nose and small mouth. A gem or a lotus bud surmounts the ushnisha, or conical cranial protuberance. The chest is massive and corpulent, the waist slim. Typical of early Chiang Saen style, the short flap of the upper garment ends above the left breast.

44 ────────

Seated Buddha image. Bronze. 87 cm high. 16-17th century. Lan Na. Although attributed to as late as the 17th century, this image is in the Early Chiang Saen style, but is comparable to the series of images dated by inscription between 1469–1565

Images of the first type have a heavy solidity of the body and give an impression of great strength and virile energy, with massive shoulders, the chest inflated as if with yogic breath, and a slim waistline. Typically, surmounting the conical ushnisha or supernatural protuberance of the skull is a knob-like finial, perhaps a lotus bud or a gem, thought to have derived from contacts with India. Below the prominent curl-covered hairline, the face is round and fleshy, almost sensual. The massive, almost corpulent body is clothed in a robe worn in the open mode, and the flap of the robe is short, ending above the left breast. The right hand touches the right knee in the mudra of Victory over Mara. Adding to the impression of restrained strength, the legs are crossed, with the ankles locked in full lotus position, the soles of the feet pointing upwards. Images of this type are invariably seated on bases decorated with lotus petals and stamens. This decorative effect further emphasizes the virile simplicity of the image itself.

The finding o1 more images of this type but with dates ranging from 1469 to 1565 inscribed on their bases has led to controversy as to whether the undated but putatively earlier images in the Chiang Saen style are in fact contemporaneous with these later dated images. However, some scholars suggest that the differences in aesthetic and modelling between the two types reflect a difference in time, and that the dated images may have been derived from a Pala type in India that was popular between the 8th to 12th centuries. According to chronicles, devout Buddhists from the Lan Na Thai Kingdom went to the great Mahabodhi Temple in India during the reign of King Tiloka in the mid-15th century. Perhaps the Pala type Buddha images might have been introduced to Lan Na at this time.

46

Reliquary casket in the form of a Deer. Stone and gold 4.6 cm high. 16th century. Lan Na. Found at Hod. Chiang Mai.
The head of the crouching deer, turned towards the left, has a golden mask. The legs are also covered with gold. The cavity on the animal's back, intended to enshrine relics of the Buddha, has an elaborately decorated lid in gold.

45

Caparisoned Elephant. Bronze. 42.5 cm high. 19th century, Lan Na.
The caparisoned elephant with its fine decorative details has a crowned rider seated behind the howdah, which holds a lotus-bud shaped offering jar.

47

Lustral water vessel in the shape of a Hamsa, or Celestial Goose. Bronze. 20 cm high 19th century, Lan Na.
This bronze water vessel in the form of hamsa must have been made for ritual or ceremonial use.

From the mid-15th century onward, contact with Sukhothai led to Lan Na Thai images being made slimmer of body. The face became more elongated and oval, and the Sukhothai flame rather than the lotus, in time surmounted the ushnisha. The short flap of the robe gave way to an elongated one that terminated above the waistline instead of the breast. Images with these characteristics are known as the Late Chiang Saen or Chiang Mai type.

During the 16th century, crowned Buddha images in royal attire appeared in Lan Na Thai art. Generally it was only in Mahayana Buddhism that images were crowned. As the kingdom followed the austere Theravada sect of Hinayana Buddhism, these crowned images are taken to represent the

48

Seated Buddha. Bronze. 67.5 cm high. 15–16th century. Late Chiang Saen or Chiang Mai style, Lan Na.

The Buddha is seated on a lotus pedestal base in folded-leg posture and performs the mudra of Victory over Mara. In comparison to the Early Chiang Saen, this type of image shows Sukothai influence in the flame-shaped halo, the folded posture of the legs, and the long flap of the upper garment ending at the navel.

49

Miniature Shrine. Gilded metal. 45 cm high. 16th century. Lan Na. Found at Hod. Chiang Mai.
This magnificent miniature shrine reveals a glimpse of the kingdom's architectural grandeur and richness in the 16th century. At each corner of the shrine is a deva or celestial being holding a lotus.

Buddha Sakyamuni in imperial disguise humbling the deluded and proud King Jambupati. This legend appears only in Southeast Asia.

The richness and grandeur of the early Lan Na Thai Kingdom, which flourished up to the Burmese conquest of the north in 1556, is also reflected in its handsome gilded miniature objects of art. Many such exquisite objects were unearthed from the ruined chedis of Hod in Chiang Mai Province in 1960 by archaeologists of the Fine Arts Department. The magnificent collection includes Buddhist votive objects, some on elaborately carved bases holding ornamental regalia, and also miniature specimens of Lan Na religious architecture, as well as animal figurines such as elephants, deer, goats, frogs, ducks and two-headed birds. ■

50 ━━━━━━

Crowned Buddha. Bronze. 62 cm high. 15–16th Century, Late Chiang Saen or Chiang Mai style, Lan Na.

Crowned Buddha images had frequently been represented in Pala India during the 11th century. However, this type of image in Hinayana Buddhist countries in Southeast Asia is taken to portray the historical Buddha in imperial disguise humbling the deluded and proud King Jambupati. The complete royal attire includes a diadem, earrings, necklaces, armlets, bracelets, finger-rings and anklets.

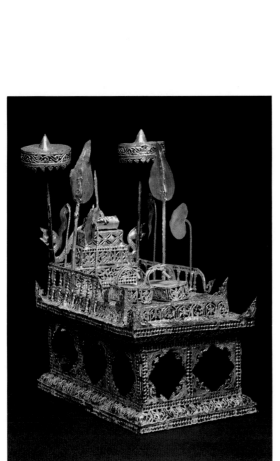

51 ━━━━━━

Replica of Regalia. Gilded Metal. 16.5 cm high. 16th century. Lan Na. Found at Hod, Chiang Mai.

Arranged on an elaborate pedestal this model of regalia comprises a throne, umbrellas, fans, fly-whisks and a pair of fine filigree sandals. Miniature votive objects such as this are believed to have been made to be enshrined inside a chedi or as offerings following cremation.

Sukhothai Sculpture

The origins of the Thai people are shrouded in legend. Current scholarly debate questions traditionally held beliefs that they had migrated over the centuries (prior to the thirteenth century) into northern and upper central Thailand, possibly from regions of Southern China, and perhaps areas further east or north. However, it is with these people in the Sukhothai region and their rise to greatness that the history of Thailand, or Siam, is said to have begun.

Until the middle of the 13th century A.D. regions of what today are northeast and central Thailand were under Khmer rule. At that time, at Sukhothai, a group of independent Thai chieftains who owed allegiance to the Khmer were able to throw off the Khmer yoke and establish themselves as rulers.

Although this kingdom of Sukhothai (translated as 'The Dawn of Happiness') enjoyed only a brief period of independent flowering – less than 200 years before it was absorbed in 1438 by the power of Ayutthaya of the central plains – it is regarded by the Thais as a Golden Age, the fount of traditions still practised today.

Sukhothai and its regional towns reveal that although the Hindu beliefs of the banished Khmer were partially retained, it was the Buddhist faith that gave impetus to the new civilisation. The third King of Sukhothai, Ramkhamhaeng, regarded by Thais as the father of the nation and creator of the Thai alphabet, records on his 1292 inscription the abundant prosperity and religious piety of the people who flock to numerous Buddhist Sanctuaries, both inside and outside the city walls.

While Sukhothai architecture reveals a harmonious synthesis of various regional influences, the sculpture of the period is a unique expression of religious vitality, abounding as it does with radiant otherworldly images both in stucco and bronze. In the casting of bronze Buddha and Hindu images, the craftsmen of Sukhothai are unsurpassed.

To the uninitiated eye Sukhothai period Buddha images may at first appear awkward and distorted. This 'distortion' is deliberate, as sculptors did not base their images on human models but on close and literal interpretations of metaphors from religious verse and Pali language scriptures, which specified the many distinguishing marks or *lakshanas* of the Great Being. Accordingly, the artist created images that were intended to reflect the superhuman spiritual and compassionate nature of the Buddha.

52 ▪ 53

Ramkhamhaeng stele. And detail of Thai script. Stone, 4-sided. 109 cm high. 13th century, Sukhothai.
This obelisk was found at Sukhothai in 1833 by the then prince-monk who was to become King Mongkut (Rama IV) from 1851-1868. The inscription, parts of which appear to have been composed by the **great King Ramkhamhaeng describes life** *in the kingdom of the 'Dawn of Happiness', and is the first extant inscription firmly identified as using Thai script, traditionally said by the Thais to have been devised by King Ramkhamhaeng.*

Characteristically, classic Sukh-othai images are seated on a plain base, with the right hand placed near the knee, performing the gesture of Calling the Earth to Witness or Victory over Mara, representing the moment of Enlightenment. Soaring above the ush-nisha or skull protuberance is a Sukhothai innovation, the Thai flame, symbolising the Buddha's radiant spiritual energy. The hair-line forms a delicate V-shape at the top of the brow. This shape is echoed by the curved sweep of the arched eyebrows which join at the bridge of a substantial almost hooked nose, shaped like 'a par-rot's beak' according to the scriptures. Three lines incised at the neck are also marks of the Great Being, as are the elongated earlobes denoting the Buddha's former princely status. The shoulders of Sukhothai images are extremely broad, and the chest in-flated, as if with yogic breath. As stipulated in the scriptures, the arms are long and sinuous, 'like the trunk of a young elephant.' This convention is particularly evi-dent in the images of the Walking Buddha in the full round, a Sukho-thai innovation.

Bronze images of the Hindu gods were also cast during Suk-hothai times. In anatomical pro-portions they closely resemble the Buddha images. However, the Hindu gods are crowned and wear royal attire, being cult objects in royal court rituals performed by Brahmin priests. ■

54 ▬▬▬▬▬▬▬
Seated Buddha image. Bronze. 68 cm high. 14th century. Sukhothai.
This serene red-lacquered and gilded bronze image displays the hallmarks of classical Sukhothai style, which aimed not at naturalistic expression but a spi-ritual ideal. The robe, with its characte-ristic 'fishtail' notch at the navel, ap-pears diaphanous, being outlined by ridges at the breast, ankles and wrist. The delicately modelled hands and fingers 'like lotus buds opening' per-form the action of Calling the Earth to Witness, signifying Victory over Mara, or Delusion, and attainment of Enlight-enment. Typically, the legs are not crossed but folded gently, contributing to the grace of the image.

▬▬▬▬▬▬▬▬▬▬▬▬▬

40

55 ━━━━━━━━━━━

Profile of seated Buddha image. Bronze. 105 cm high (whole image). 14-15th century, Sukhothai. Clearly evident here are the Sukhothai characteristics: an oval shaped head, with large haircurls, topped by the flame of radiant energy; eyes like half opened lotus buds; a substantial nose ' hooked like a parrot's beak ', incised gently smiling mouth; rounded and incised chin like a lime or mango stone. The elongated earlobes reflect the Buddha's former princely status while the three lines at the neck are considered marks of beauty in a Great Being.

56 ━━━━━━━━━━━

Walking Buddha. Bronze. 60.5 cm high. 15th century. Sukhothai.

Walking images in the full round were an innovation of the Sukhothai period. This image performs the abhaya mudra, or gesture of Dispelling Fear. Characteristic of the period are the broad shoulders and pendant arm ' like the trunk of a young elephant '. The flat feet and projecting heels are part of the anatomy characteristic of a Great Being.

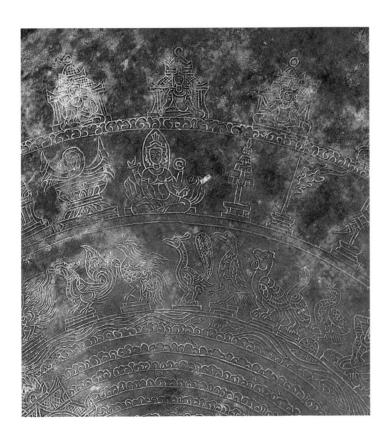

57
Detail of the Wheel at the center of the footprint.

58

Buddha Footprint. Bronze. 156 cm long.
105 cm wide. 15th century. Sukhothai.
In early Buddhist art in India, aniconic
symbols represented the life and the
teachings of the Buddha. While the
Wheel symbolised the teachings, the
footprint represented the presence of
the Buddha, or the idea of his teachings
having travelled to a specific place.
Bronze representations of the Buddha
footprint were venerated during the
Sukhothai period. At the centre of this
footprint is incised the Wheel of the
Law. Inscribed in the wheel are many of
the 108 auspicious signs listed in Pali
language scriptures as ' lakshanas ' or
characteristics of the Great Being.
Concentric circles of wave-like design
represent the seven ocean-fringed
mountains at the centre of which is
Mount Meru, the centre of the Universe
in Buddhist Cosmology. At the outer
edges, graceful deities pay homage to
the teachings. Bordering the footprint
are walking Buddha images and
Buddhist disciples.

59

Uma. Bronze. 146 cm high. 14th century. Sukhothai.

Uma, the wife of the Hindu god Shiva, is dressed in royal court attire of the Sukhothai period. The necklet, armbands and crown are embellished with gold paint. While the right hand held a now vanished object, the left shoulder and arm display the modelling techniques common to Buddha images, being shaped 'like the trunk of a young elephant'

60

Detail of Uma.

61

Vishnu. Bronze. 267 cm high. 14th century. Sukhothai.

Standing on a lotus pedestal, this monumental image of the Hindu god Vishnu replicates the bodily proportions of Buddha images of the time. However, crowned, wearing royal attire and still bearing some of the attributes of the god, (conch shell, discus or chakra), the image clearly represents the Preserver of the Universe.

62

Phra Buddha Sihing. Bronze plated with gold. 166 cm high, including throne pedestal, mid 15th century. This serenely beautiful image is highly venerated in Thailand, being regarded as second in importance only to the Emerald Buddha. Many interesting and perhaps apocryphal legends surround the image which presides over the Buddhaisawan Chapel in the National Museum grounds, formerly the Palace of the Second King. Each Thai New Year, the image is carried in procession to the Pramane Grounds where the faithful may make merit by pouring lustral water on the image.

Adding credence to legends and stories from ancient chronicles that the image may have originated in Sri Lanka is the fact that the hands of the image are in the position for meditation, unusual in Thai art but common in Sri Lankan images. However, the image incorporates Thai characteristics of the Chiang Saen and Sukhothai style: the former include the lotus and stamen decorated base; the latter in general features that include the legs in a gentle folded position, as well as the Sukhothai flame above the ushnisha or cranial protuberance.

U Thong Sculpture

In 1350 King U Thong established the kingdom of Ayutthaya, which was to become one of the most important and long-lasting kingdoms on the mainland of Southeast Asia. The kingdom was situated in the Menam (or Chao Phraya) basin, previously occupied by the Dvaravati kingdom and then by the Khmer, and was to the south of its political rival, Sukhothai. The name U Thong has been used to designate the art which flourished in this central plains area of Thailand from the 12th century until approximately the 15th century.

63 ━━━━━━━━━━━━━

Seated Buddha image. Bronze. 103 cm high. 13–14th century, U Thong style, Early Ayutthaya. Typical of the U Thong style is the band delineating the hairline, the angularity of the body, and the concave base on which the image is seated. However, the large incised conical ushnisha and the curved robe flap terminating in an almost fishtail notch indicate a transitional style.

Many images in the U Thong style predate the founding of the Ayutthaya kingdom. The earliest images date from the 12th century, but are usually incorporated by scholars into the Early Ayutthaya period. The U Thong style of Buddha image is divided into three different phases called by art historians A, B, and C. Type A is the earliest (12th to 13th century), with types B and C somewhat overlapping in time (type B spans the 13th to 14th century, while type C dates from the 13th to the 15th century)

Features common to almost all three types include a small band between the hairline and forehead, the robe draped in the open mode with a long flap from the left shoulder ending in a straight line above the navel. All have fingers of unequal length. The head is covered with small sometimes spiky curls. The images are generally seated, with the legs folded, on a simple concave base and perform the gesture of Subduing Mara or Calling the Earth to Witness. Bronze was the favoured medium, although stucco and sandstone images were also made.

The faces of early U Thong images are square and show a mixture of Mon and Khmer characteristics. In later images, oval faces are the result of Sukhothai influence, which was to prevail. In U Thong A images the ushnisha or cranial protuberance is usually surmounted by a lotus bud. In styles B and C, this is replaced by an elongated flame. Similarly, the silhouette of the images of this time also becomes elongated through Sukhothai influence. Graceful and slender, images of the U Thong C style were produced in great numbers and were to influence images of the whole Ayutthaya period. ■

2. From the mid-15th century until 17th century, the Sukhothai influence prevailed, but U Thong C characteristics were evident. The facial expression changed. The smile became very faint or non-existent, and often the expression was stern. The bases of images became more decorated, occasionally illustrating episodes in the life of the Buddha (fig.72)

3. In the 17th century, during the reign of King Prasat Thong (1629–1656), when the Khmer again became vassals of Ayut-thaya, their artistic style became fashionable and was imitated by Thai artists. Consequently, sands-tone images enjoyed a renewed popularity. In keeping with Khmer tradition, the eyes and lips are incised, and occasionally above the lips there is a faint moustache. However, the oval face and the flame on the ushnisha make the image distinctly Thai.

4. From the 17th century until 1767, during the Late Ayutthaya period, crowned Buddha images were popular. These had existed previously, but generally until the 17th century the Buddha, if crowned, was still depicted wearing a simple monastic robe. After that time the robe was increasingly ornamented. During the 17th century it seems that as the splendor of Ayutthaya increased, Buddha images, to reflect that splendor, became more ornately adorned. The headdress became taller and more elaborate, with decorative wing-like ornaments extending behind the ears, which were enhanced by earrings. Jewels fashionable during each particular reign were added around the neck, on the arms, and across the chest (fig.74). By the end of the 17th century embroidery-like patterns and ornamentation decorated the Buddha's originally simple robe. In keeping with the majesty of royal garb, the facial expressions were stern and solemn. ∎

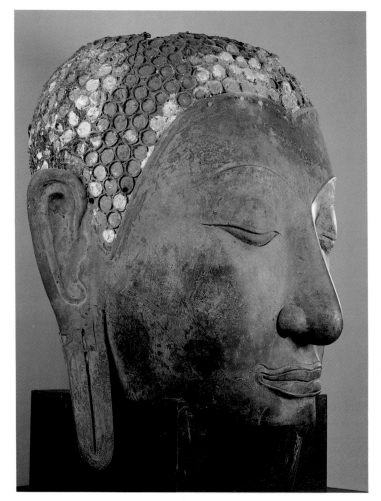

68 ▬▬▬▬▬▬▬
Head of a Buddha image. Bronze. 112 cm long. 15–16th century, Ayutthaya. This monumental head is remarkable for its serene spirituality. Incised above the lips is the faint suggestion of a moustache. Stucco, lacquered and gilded hair curls originally adorned the bronze coiffure.

69

Buddha head. Stone 56 cm high. Ayutthaya style. Ayutthaya's power in Angkor in the 14th and 17th centuries led to assimilation of Khmer ideas by the Thai in their architecture and art of those periods. Thus, while the features of this head are primarily in the Thai style, the use of sandstone as a medium, and the incision of a moustache above the lips denote Khmer influence.

70

Votive tablet mould. Lacquered and gilded metal. 20 cm high. Ayutthaya. Surrounded by seated Buddha images subduing Mara, set in a niche at the center is a Walking Buddha image reminiscent of the Sukhothai period.

71

Reclining Buddha image. Bronze. 32 cm long. 15-16th century, Ayutthaya. Reclining images of the Buddha generally symbolise the death of the Buddha and Parinirvana, the ultimate aim of Buddhism, ending the cycles of rebirth. Traditionally, reclining images, in spite of the law of gravity, display the lower part of the robe 'levitating', or extending from the body as it would be on a standing image.

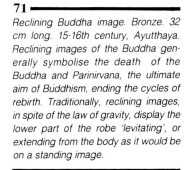

72

Seated Buddha Subduing Mara. Bronze. 56 cm high. 14-16th century. Ayutthaya. This sculpture and detail of base represents the episode of the Enlightenment of the Buddha. Confronted by Mara (symbolising evil) and his demon army, Gautama or the Buddha-to-be must prove his claim to a perfect state of virtue. Pointing to the earth with his right hand. Gautama replies: "The earth shall be my witness." The goddess of the Earth, Thoranee, who has witnessed all the merits accumulated by the Buddha-to-be in his previous lives, wrings out her hair, wet with lustral water ritually poured onto the ground during each of the innumerable meritorious deeds of the Buddha-to-be in his former lives. This provides a deluge which drowns Mara's army, washing away the demons of delusion, ignorance and attachment, symbolising the moment when Gautama becomes the Buddha or Enlightened One. This is a popular theme in mural painting, but rather rarely seen fully depicted in sculpture. On the base, Thoranee is in the centre.

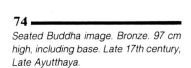

73

Crowned Standing Buddha image. Bronze. 72 cm high. 17-18th century, Late Ayutthaya.

Characteristic of the Ayutthaya period is the finely worked diadem, with 'hinges' protruding above the ears which are adorned with inverted lotus Khmer style earrings. The monastic robe covers both shoulders in the Lopburi style and has a simplified belt and frontal flap. The curve of the pendant arm reflects Sukhothai influence. The image performs the gesture of Dispelling Fear.

74

Seated Buddha image. Bronze. 97 cm high, including base. Late 17th century, Late Ayutthaya.

Highly adorned images reflected the royal attire of the Ayutthaya kings. Superimposed on the monastic robe, itself decorated by embroidery designs at the borders, are elaborately intricate armlets, and double baldric crossed at the chest. The tapering lavish headdress supports long pendants hung behind the ears.

Ratanakosin Sculpture

After the destruction of Ayutthaya by the Burmese in 1767, a new kingdom was founded in Thonburi under King Taksin. Subsequently, in 1782, the capital was moved to Bangkok, with the foundation of the Chakri dynasty, whose kings are known retrospectively by the title 'Rama'. The art of this time, from 1782 until the present is known as the Bangkok or Ratanakosin style.

The art of the Bangkok period can be divided into two distinct artistic eras. The earlier era spans the reigns of King Rama I to King Rama III (1782-1851) and embraces classical Siamese traditions. The latter era dates from the reign of King Rama IV to the present, incorporating both classical and modern westernized elements.

During the early Bangkok period as many as 1,200 extant images were brought down to Bangkok from war-torn areas of central and northern Thailand and were installed in the city's new monasteries. Artists vied to create lofty and ornate thrones for them. Consequently, relatively few images were made during that period. New images, when made, were either cast in bronze or carved from wood, and generally followed the Ayutthaya traditions of Buddha image-making. These can barely be distinguished from their earlier prototypes. Though some were plain, many of these early Bangkok period images were elaborately decorated, with artists striving to outdo their predecessors in abundant ornamentation. Thus the originally simple monk's robe apparel of the image was entirely decorated with embroidery-like designs, and heavy ornate bands embellished the edges of the robes. Crowned Buddha images were also popular at this time, dressed in ceremonial vestments designed to resemble royal attire. These were extremely ornate, heavily decorated and bejewelled, with crown-like headdresses tapering to a pointed spire-like finial. The refinement and simplicity of Buddha images made in earlier periods gave way to regal ornamentation and, some would say, a loss of spirituality in the image.

During the reign of King Rama III, images of the Buddha were commissioned depicting thirty-four new attitudes, all drawn from important events in the life of the Buddha. However, the new atti-

75

Ceremonial candle holder. Gilt bronze. 20 cm high. 19th century, Bangkok period. One of a set depicting the gods of the nine planets, this utensil was used in religious circumambulatory ceremonies. At the centre of the stylised Boddhi leaf light reflector is depicted the Hindu god Vishnu riding his vehicle the Garuda.

tudes proved unpopular and the six traditional attitudes remain the most common.

Later Bangkok period sculpture of the Buddha became more realistic and humanized, seeking historical accuracy. This resulted from the influence of King Rama IV (1851-1868) whose interest in the Sciences and rational thinking led him to eliminate elements of the supernatural in Buddhism. Consequently, images favoured by King Rama IV were unusual in that they lacked many of the supernatural attributes, including the cranial protuberance or ushnisha. In this humanizing tradition another unusual image of this later period, commissioned by King Rama V (1868-1910), is the standing Gandhara style Buddha in the gesture of Calling Down the Rain. The distinctly humanized and western anatomy and hair style, the pleated toga-like robe, all reminiscent of

the Indian Gandhara style (1-3 century A.D.), epitomise the quest for historical accuracy.

Other sculpture of the Bangkok period includes disciples, ascetics, rishis or hermits in yoga positions, Hindu divinities, guardians and mythical creatures from the Buddhist cosmology. ■

76

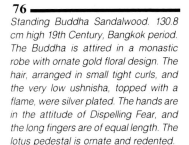

Standing Buddha Sandalwood. 130.8 cm high 19th Century, Bangkok period. The Buddha is attired in a monastic robe with ornate gold floral design. The hair, arranged in small tight curls, and the very low ushnisha, topped with a flame, were silver plated. The hands are in the attitude of Dispelling Fear, and the long fingers are of equal length. The lotus pedestal is ornate and redented.

77

Standing Gandhara style Buddha image. Bronze. 73.7 cm high Early 20th century. Bangkok period.
This is a naturalistic Buddha image modeled after the Indian Gandhara period images of the 1st to 3rd century. The robe is pleated in the Gandhara style and the hair is arranged in the Greco-Roman style of that period. The right hand is raised to shoulder level, fingers half open in the attitude of Calling Down the Rain. Commissioned by King Rama V, the image is a blend of Thai and Western art, visible in the European anatomy of the Buddha.

78

Crowned Standing Buddha with Royal Attire Bronze. 248 cm. high. 19th Century, Bangkok period.
The Buddha image on a lotus pedestal is dressed in ornamental royal attire. The garment shows fine details of embroidery. The headdress has a diadem and high tapered mukuta. The hands are in the abhaya mudra or Dispelling Fear, popular in the Bangkok period.

Miniature Bronze Statues Depicting Events in the Life of the Buddha. This group of bronze miniatures is from a set of twenty-nine miniatures depicting the main events in the Buddha's life, from birth to Mahaparinirvana – the great total extinction of the Buddha. Sculpted during the reign of King Rama III (1824-51), these miniatures capture the vitality and piety of each event. They were part of the Royal Collection in the Grand Palace.

79

Birth Scene, 7.3 cm high, 3.5 cm long. Queen Mahamaya holds on to the sal tree while the future Buddha emerges from her side. The five-tiered umbrella indicates his princely rank.

80

The Great Departure. 6.5 cm high, 7 cm long.
Prince Siddhartha leaves his home at night after deciding to become an ascetic. His faithful groom stands by his side. Evil Mara blocks the way temporarily, symbolizing Siddhartha's last-minute doubts.

81

Cutting of the Hair. 5.5 cm high, 9.2 cm long.
Prince Siddhartha renounces the world by cutting off his hair which is collected by divinites as relics. His groom and horse are filled with grief.

82

Indra and the three Stringed Lute. 4 cm high, 6.5. cm long. Siddhartha, now Gautama the ascetic, fasts until near death. Indra demonstrates, with a three-stringed lute that neither the loose nor the rigid ways of life are correct, but only the middle path, between extremes, will lead to understanding, and Enlightenment,

83

Victory Over Mara. 15.5 cm high, 15.8 cm long.
Also known as the scene of Enlightenment. Buddha (missing here), meditating under the Bodhi tree, was challenged by Mara, upon which he called the Earth to be witness to all his virtues. Toranee, the Earth goddess, in response collected the lustral water of his virtues in her hair and drowned the army of Mara (on the left). Crown and tree are decorated with gold leaf and semi-precious stones.

Ceramics

Discoveries in the past two decades and recent archaeological research have contributed greatly towards understanding the history of ceramic production in Thailand. In the mid-1960s, a fortuitous find of an undisturbed repository of Ban Chiang pottery on the northern Khorat Plateau in northeastern Thailand instigated a series of surveys that revealed an extensive prehistoric civilization.

In the mid-1970s significant ceramic data were found in three areas. First, several ancient sunken cargo ships carrying Thai ceramics were sited in the Gulf of Thailand. Quantities of glazed stoneware vessels were brought to the surface for analysis. These maritime finds establish that the production of Thai ceramics most likely continued for a longer period of time than was previously believed. Additionally, these finds help to identify Thailand's early maritime activity and trade routes. Second, the excavation of a Khmer kiln and the discovery of over one hundred kiln mounds in Buriram Province in northeastern Thailand, substantiate that the area was a major production center for Khmer ceramics. Third, the identification of hundreds of kilns in northern Thailand confirms the existence of an extensive ceramic industry operating between the 14th and late 16th centuries.

In the 1980s, evidence of ancient ceramic production in Thailand is continuing to materialize and expand. Currently, ceramic excavations are taking place in north central Thailand at Si Satchanalai, approximately 70 kilometers north of Sukhothai, where Sawankhalok wares were produced at Ban Ko Noi, the main ceramic production site. Finds include a progressive development in kiln design starting from a simple bank kiln. They also verify an indigenous

evolution in technology, which was previously believed to have been imported. Additionally, archaeological research suggests that the production of glazed stonewares in Thailand began at Si Satchanalai, perhaps as early as the 10th century rather than the 14th century, a previously established date. Also, sufficient evidence has emerged to confirm that the dark glazed monochromes previously incorrectly identified as 'Chalieng Ware' were made at Si Satchanalai.

The excavation of an ancient kiln at Phitsanulok in north central Thailand adds another link to the disclosure of Thailand's ceramic history. An estimated 40-50 kilns situated on the bank of the Nan River produced wheel thrown, utilitarian earthenwares and stonewares. Although the vessels were undoubtedly made primarily for local use, at least some of the wares were transported by river to Ayutthaya, as they have been found on board the sunken ships in the Gulf of Thailand.

In early 1984, a previously unknown ceramic site was discovered in Nan Province. A test excavation revealed kilns that produced distinctive glazed stonewares with a preliminary date of the late 15th or early 16th century.

In late 1984, an enormous cache of ceramics was discovered in hilltop burial sites which seem to date between the mid-14th and

mid-16th centuries and are situated in the mountainous terrain of Tak Province, north central Thailand. Types include Chinese, Sukhothai, Sawankhalok, Northern Thai, Haripunchai, some Vietnamese and several unknown types. A similar find of primarily Northern Thai wares was made in early 1985 in the Om Koi area of Chiang Mai Province. These unprecedented finds present a plethora of questions particularly regarding who used these wares. Although the production of Haripunchai wares in the Lamphun area, Northern Thailand, has been known for some time, it is only recently that a later, unrelated production period has been discovered. Hundreds of earthenware water bottles found at Tak and surface shards in the Lamphun area indicate a 14th to 16th century date.

Knowledge of Thailand's ceramic past is increasing with each discovery. On-the-site research and scientific analysis is expanding under the direction of the Fine Arts Department of Thailand. The National Museum's eagerness to bring the latest archaeological finds to the public is reflected in continuing additions and special exhibitions as new discoveries are made. Precise identification of all the ancient ceramic production sites, their chronology and interrelationships are the goals and hopes of the future.

The ceramic collection of the Bangkok National Museum comprises over 3,000 pieces spanning 6,000 years, from prehistory to the 20th century. The strength of the collection is its comprehensive range of domestic wares.

Thailand's prehistoric pottery is

collectively referred to as "The Ban Chiang Cultural Tradition," named after a village in northeastern Thailand which is the type site for the majority of wares. The most recent scientific testing results conclude that the prehistoric Ban Chiang culture extends from about 3,600 B.C. to around A.D. 200-300. However, the bronze and iron artifacts that have been found in association with pottery represent the products of a highly developed metal industry. It is possible that additional discoveries may produce an earlier date for the beginning of prehistory in Thailand.

Typical wares of the Early Period of Ban Chiang are coil built vessels finished with an anvil and beater. The varied tones of the earthenware clay are a result of uneven firing conditions and establish the use of a simple, open-fire pit. A distinctive feature of the Early Period vessels is a band of clay applied around the mid-section (fig.87).

The Late Period wares are characterized by a dark clay covered with a buff slip and painted with red geometric designs (fig. 86). The Ban Chiang cultural tradition was initially identified by the discovery of shards from this period.

The prehistoric period ended in the beginning centuries of the Christian era. Practically no ceramic finds in Thailand can be confidently dated to the next 500 years. But, similarities with some prehistoric shapes, techniques and decorations can be found in early pottery produced in central Thailand during the Dvaravati Period (7th-11th century). This important evidence supports the theory of a continuous occupation in central Thailand between the two periods.

Later Dvaravati pottery includes unglazed earthenwares that closely resemble Indian pottery in form and design.

Northeastern Thailand was a major production area for Khmer, or Lopburi, ceramics between the 11th and 12th centuries. Basic materials and techniques were used to produce vessels for utilitarian and religious use. An exceptionally fine example of the Khmer appreciation of nature is a predominantly brown glazed elephant standing on four short legs, with modeled trunk, ears and facial features (fig.89). Interestingly, the tusks are green glazed, indicating careful attention to detail.

As the Khmer presence in Thailand diminished in the 12th century some theories hold that scattered groups of Thais migrated into the area. They formed principalities which expanded in size,

84

A stoneware jar presumably used for storing water. The bulbous-shaped body has a sloping shoulder, short neck and everted, rounded mouth rim. The glaze color ranges from dark brown to yellowish. Date: 14-15 C; Period: Sawankhalok; Provenance: Unknown. Dimensions: ht: 90 cm.

85

An unglazed, earthenware tripod derived from a metal form. Three perforated, conical-shaped legs support a carinate body with a wide mouth and flaring rim. The smooth surface of the upper body is burnished; the lower body and legs are cord-marked. Date Prehistoric: Provenance: Ban Kao, Kanchanaburi Province Dimensions: ht: 22 cm.

86

A buff-colored, earthenware pot with wide mouth, flaring rim and round bottom. The red-painted swirling bands are characteristic of Late Period vessels found at Ban Chiang. Date: Late Period, ca. 300 BC – AD 100 (Ref: White. Ban Chiang); Period: Prehistoric; Provenance: Ban Chiang. Dimensions: ht: 44.0 cm.

87

*An unglazed, medium-sized earthen-
ware pot with a wide mouth, short foot,
and band applied around the mid-
section. The upper body is incised with
a geometric design; the lower body is
cord-marked. The color of the coarse
clay varies from gray to black. Date:
Early Period ca. 3600-2500 B.C., (Ref:
White. Ban Chiang); Period: Prehistoric;
Provenance: Ban Chiang. Dimensions:
ht: 18.3 cm.*

strengthened gradually in power, and in time culminated in the establishment of several Thai strongholds. The first Thai Kingdom was established at Sukhothai, in north central Thailand, in the mid-13th century.

Thailand is recognized internationally for a wide range of appealing glazed stonewares which were produced at two main centers–Sukhothai and Si Satchanalai in north central Thailand. The earliest glazed wares were produced at Si Satchanalai and include a broad range of shapes. They were most commonly decorated by using a sgraffito technique and a green colored glaze. These wares were the prototype for the later celadon glaze.

Production at Sukhothai began in the 13th century or later. Shapes include primarily plates, bowls and pots. Weighty and robust, the forms were potted from a grainy clay with impurities. A light-colored slip over the body provided a light background for the iron-black designs that were freely painted on the surface. Perhaps the most typical motif is the ubiquitous fish (fig. 93). A superb example of Sukhothai craftsmanship in the Museum Collection is a large bowl with cover (fig. 97). Well-executed geometric patterns mingle with indigenous floral designs. The lotus bud finial on the cover is typically Thai.

Architectural fixtures such as finials, tiles, railings and balu-

strades were made at Si Satchanalai beginning in the 13th or 14th century, for use on religious buildings and grounds. The Museum Collection contains a substantial representation of these wares. The skill of the Thai potters in sculpting ceramic objects is apparent in the museum examples (fig. 92, 94, 102).

In the mid-14th century, China's prohibition of overseas trade opened up a vast export market for the Thais, who developed new shapes and glazes for export, primarily to other parts of Southeast Asia. The wares reflect the vitality and creativeness of Thai potters. They have a distinct character and express a sensitivity that seems to have eluded the more technically developed ceramics.

The crest of potting technology was achieved in the production of Sawankhalok celadons at Ban Ko Noi. Jars, pots and plates with a lustrous, jade-like green glaze are so admired today that the craft of making celadons has been revived at several modern factories in Thailand.

While the Kingdom of Sukhothai was extending its boundaries to the south, other groups of Thais were setting up strongholds in the north. Lan Na Thai, or northern Thailand, reached its peak in the 15th century and included Chiang Mai, Chiang Rai, Payao and Lampang. A creditable range of monochromes and decorated wares was produced in these areas for the utilitarian and religious needs of the local population. Fig. 103, a two-color storage jar, is a typical example of Northern Thai ceramics.

As the glory of the kingdoms in northern Thailand faded, the demand for ceramics diminished and production gradually ceased. Ceramic focus shifted to the south, at Ayutthaya, the new kingdom then dominating Thailand. A special class of porcelain, made in China, between the 17th and 19th centuries exclusively for export to Thailand, dominated the ceramic field. Collectively known as 'Sino-Thai Wares', two primary types, *Bencharong* and *Lai Nam Thong*, constitute this ceramic group. Multicolored enamels were used to decorate the entire surface of white glazed vessels with intricate Thai-style designs. The earliest piece in the Museum Collection is a late 17th century bowl with mythical figures and a fire pattern enameled on a black background (fig.106). An internationally known example of *Lai Nam Thong* is a pedestal water jar with a conical-shaped cover (fig.108). The precise workmanship and carefully executed designs give this piece the distinction of having been exhibited in three foreign countries. One of the most distinctive pieces of Sino-Thai type wares is a drum (fig.107). The porcelain head is protected with split leather thongs. Enamel designs add artistic appeal to this unusual piece. It was most likely used for religious ceremonies.

Because of the extensive time span and the inclusion of domestic as well as export wares, the ceramic collection in the Bangkok National Museum is the most representative display of Thai ceramics on public exhibition. ■

88 ━━━━━━

A utilitarian jar with an oval body, sloping shoulder, short neck and narrow mouth with rim. The shoulder and upper body are incised with a loop design separated by rings. Carved rings near the base are diagnostic. The gray body is covered with a brown glaze. Date: 12 C (Ref: Rooney. Khmer Ceramics); Period: Lopburi; Provenance: Unknown. Dimensions: ht: 61 cm.

89

An elephant-shaped pot with an incised, ornamental saddle and two lug handles at each side of the opening on the back. The light-colored clay is covered with a brown glaze except for green-glazed tusks. Date: 13-14 C; Period:Lopburi;Provenance: Nakhon Ratchasima, Wat Sutthachinda. Dimensions: ht: 21 cm.

90

A gourd-shaped bottle with modeled and incised monkey   like features. Bands of dots are applied around the neck and lower body. The gray clay is covered with a homogeneous, dark brown glaze. Date: Last half 11 C, (Ref: Rooney Khmer Ceramics); Period: Lopburi; Provenance: Unknown. Dimensions: ht: 23.5 cm.

91

A brown-glazed, bird-shaped pot with groups of incised vertical lines around the body. Date: Last half 11 C (Ref: Rooney. Khmer Ceramics); Period: Lopburi; Provenance: Unknown. Dimensions: diam: 10 cm.

62

92

A stoneware, diamond-shaped architectural tile with a stylised flower applied in the center. The light colored clay is covered with a thick whitish glaze. Date: 14-15 C; Period: Sawankhalok; Provenance: Wat Srasri, Muang Kao District, Sukhothai. Dimensions: length: 32.5 cm.

93

An underglaze black plate shard with a Sukhothai fish design in the center. The light colored clay is covered with a transparent glaze. Date: 14 C; Period: Sukhothai; Provenance: Unknown. Dimensions: diam: 25.7 cm.

94

A stoneware architectural fixture modeled in the form of a mythical figure. The beady, brown-glazed eyes are in stark contrast to the white-glazed form. Date: 14-15 C; Period: Sawankhalok; Provenance: Unknown. Dimensions: ht: 28 cm.

96

A celadon stem plate with an incised flower in the center encircled by a band of vertical lines. The short pedestal with splayed foot is hollow. The vessel is covered with a homogeneous bluish-green glaze. Date: 14-15 C; Period: Sawankhalok; Provenance: Unknown. Dimensions: Diam: 10 cm.

95

An underglaze black covered box with a lotus-bud-shaped knob. Horizontal rings on the lid are repeated on the lower body and enclose a broad, vegetal scroll painted in iron black that extends over the lid and body. The unglazed gray base has a circular firing mark. Date: 14-15 C; Period: Sawankhalok; Provenance: Unknown. Dimensions: ht: 10 cm.

97

An underglaze black bowl with cover and lotus-bud-shaped handle. Geometric panels enclosing floral elements predominate. A band of comma-like strokes surround the lower body and a repetitive sunburst design encircles the handle. The buff-colored clay is speckled with whitish particles. Date: 14 C; Period: Sukhothai/Sawankhalok; Provenance: Unknown. Dimensions: ht: including lid, 21.7 cm; diameter 18.6 cm.

98

A celadon elephant with a rider seated behind a square-shaped, shallow cup. Animal features and saddle ornamentation are defined with modeling and incising. The gray clay is covered with a crackled, greenish glaze. Date: 14-15 C; Period: Sawankhalok; Provenance: Unknown. Dimensions: ht: 22 cm.

99

A celadon pot of squat form with a short neck and narrow mouth. Incised leaves enclosed by horizontal rings decorate the broad shoulder. The lustrous bluish glaze extends to the unglazed, buff-colored foot. Date: 14-15 C; Period: Sawankhalok; Provenance: Unknown; Dimensions: diam: 6 cms.

100

A modeled, celadon figure in the form of a female sitting with legs crossed and holding a pot. Models of this type were most likely ritualistic effigy figures offered to animistic spirits for protection. Date: 14-15 C; Period: Sawankhalok; Provenance: Unknown. Dimensions: ht: 15.7 cm.

101

An underglaze black vase with a curved profile, short neck and flaring base. The neck is decorated with a band of solid petals, a chrysanthemum design covers the body and the foot is encircled with lotus-bud panels. *Date: Unknown; Lan Na Thai style. Provenance: Lent by H.R.H. Prince Damrong Rajanubhab; Dimensions: ht: 33.2 cm.*

102

A roof finial modeled in the form of a mythical animal. A combination of decorating techniques creates definition on the scaly body, ornamented necklace, mane and face. An interplay of brown painting and white glaze adds textural interest. *Date; 14-15 C; Period: Sawankhalok; Provenance: Unknown. Dimensions: ht: 78 cm.*

103

A two-color jar with an oval-shaped body, a short neck and an everted mouth rim. Horizontal rings encircle the neck and outer shoulder. The rim of the mouth and two nibs on the shoulder are light green color and the remainder of the vessel is dark brown. *Date: 16-17 C. Lan Na Thai style; Provenance: Sankampaeng; Dimensions: ht: 38 cm.*

105

A lobed Bencharong stem-bowl with fluted rim. Exterior is decorated with a vertical floral design in the famille rose palette on a reddish-orange background. A European-inspired floral swag border and a rabbit fill the center medallion of the whited glazed interior. Date: 19 C; Period: Bangkok; Provenance: Presented by Rama VII in 1928; Dimensions: diam: 28.4 cm.

104

A Bencharong toh (water) jar. The oval-shaped, lobed body stands on a pedestal. Height is added by the conical-shaped cover with jeweled tip. The white background on the exterior is decorated with a vertical panel design consisting of birds and flowers in famille verte colors. A border of lotus panels encircles the pedestal. Date: 19 C; Period: Bangkok; Provenance: Unknown. Dimensions: ht: 28.2 cm.

106

A Bencharong bowl with curving sides and a slightly flared rim. The exterior is enameled with a repetitive design consisting of two mythical figures and a fire pattern on a black background. Ceramics of this period are called Thepanom Ware, based on the name of the central figure depicted on the exterior. The interior is a clear, green color with a floral border design and an open lotus in the center. Date: Late 17-Early 18 C; Period: Ayutthaya; Provenance: Un-Known. Dimensions: diam: 17.9 cm.

107

A drum with a Bencharong head and split leather thongs. The enamel design is a multi-color floral pattern. The handle of the drum is enameled with a repetitive star design on a black background. Date: Unknown; Period: Bangkok; Provenance: Unknown. Dimensions: ht: 36 cm.

108

A Lai Nam thong toh (water) jar with a pedestal and a tiered lid with a lotus-bud-shaped handle. The gold background is decorated with a multi-color floral design. Green bands encircle the tiers, pedestal and base. This piece was exhibited in the United States (1960-2); Japan (1962); and in London (1964). Date: 18-19 C; Period: Bangkok; Provenance: Unknown. Dimensions: ht: 18 cm.

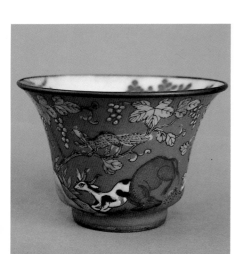

109 ▪110

An Yixing tea set with Bencharong cups enameled on the exterior and underglaze blue on the interior. The unglazed, brown clay of the teapot has been polished for a smooth surface. Each cup is decorated with a different animal of the Asian zodiac cycle on a reddish-orange background. A prunus pattern is painted in underglaze blue on the interior of the cups. Date: 19 C; Period: Bangkok; Provenance: China. Dimensions: diam 6.6 cm. (cup).

Mural Painting

The dim, cool interiors of Thai temple buildings are frequently embellished with mural paintings that depict a fabulous world of gilded palaces and pavilions, town and country landscapes in which dwell a multiplicity of beings, both real and mythical. Deriving from ancient religious texts and incorporating both Buddhist and Hindu beliefs, the tradition of Thai mural painting has as an extensive history.

Architectural remains of ancient former kingdoms provide elusive hints that paintings were employed both inside and outside religious structures. The devastation wrought by time, climate, and man's destructiveness has allowed the preservation of mere fragments, fragile relics of earlier traditions of Thai mural paintings. Surviving the destruction of Ayutthaya (1767) are some fine but relatively few examples of religious manuscripts and wall paintings. However, with the establishment first of Thonburi, and then, of Bangkok in 1782 as the capital of the new Chakri Dynasty, the arts of peace have flourished. In the ornamentation of the many temples built over succeeding decades, the art of Thai mural painting reached new heights of artistic religious expression and beauty.

Traditionally, the painting of religious scenes was regarded as an act of merit, a religious offering, and in the main, produced by anonymous artists. Temple murals were not conceived as mere decorations, but served a didactic purpose: to teach both monks and lay people moral lessons through vividly graphic narrative scenes. Most frequently portrayed are events from the Life of the historical Buddha, or from the Jataka Tales, the Buddha's Former Lives, in which are embodied the many virtues towards which people should strive.

To enable the devotee to recognise scenes of significance, certain conventions are constant throughout Thai mural painting. From the multitudes of figures crowding the landscape, the Buddha is easily recognisable by his golden skin and red robes. Royal personages, bejewelled and serene, are delineated in graceful stylised postures that reflect the arts of shadow play and the masked dance. Humbler beings going about their daily business are considerably less refined in appearance and realistically depict the life of ordinary people of the times. Here and there, depending on the occasion, fly gods and celestial beings, while demons, sacred serpents and lithe mythical creatures, half-human half-fabulous beast, merge with the foliage or float improbably on strange oceans. This blending of the real and mythical gives Thai painting its particular charm, and also reflects traditions of Buddhist and Hindu cosmology, which peoples the known world with beings from various celestial regions, allegories for states of being attained through meritorious rebirth and spiritual excellence.

In Thai mural tradition, this easily recognisable vocabulary of

111

Detail of 112. Seated below and to the right of the King are the Hindu gods, Brahma (with 4 faces) and Indra (colored green). (48 cm high, 48 cm long. Late 18th century).

beings has been relatively constant but their arrangement and emphasis has varied depending on the style favoured at the time, and materials available. During the Ayutthaya period, wall paintings were generally pastel in tone, on pale backgrounds, as the paints were made from natural earths, minerals and plants. Rows or registers of Buddhas or celestial beings predominated, with miniature vignettes here and there adding to the general effect. During the Bangkok period, a layout encompassing these traditions as well as more recent innovations evolved. With paints imported from China, vibrant colours and an abundance of gold embellishment against a dark background exemplify the best traditions of Bangkok period mural painting.

The layout common to most Bangkok period temples is clearly evident in the impressive late 18th century murals in the Buddhaisawan Chapel, which stands in the grounds of the Bangkok National Museum. Within the Chapel, from above the windows to the ceiling, are registers of celestial beings and converted demons paying graceful homage to the teachings of the Buddha. Panels between the windows feature a multiplicity of religious scenes from the Life of the Buddha. Minute and detailed descriptions of the everyday life of the people blend with scenes of religious significance. Events within the panels are divided by architecture, landscape and the occasional spectacular zigzag device that highlights in red a particularly important event. A total lack of perspective, in the Western sense, a hallmark of classical Thai mural painting, adds to the charm and almost shadow play quality of the whole. Depicting peripheral and main events in the life of the Buddha, such scenes are repeated in temple buildings past and present, all over Thailand, with varying degrees of refinement and skill. ∎

112

Highlighted by a characteristic red zig zag, within a Royal Pavilion, guests and musicians are assembled for the wedding of King Sudhodana and Princess Mahamaya (at center to left and right). They will become the parents of the being who becomes the Buddha. (224 cm high, 165 cm long. Late 18th century).

113

Detail of musicians at the wedding.

114

Rejecting extreme asceticism, Gautama, having eaten to restore himself, casts his food bowl in the waters of a river, at the bottom of which is depicted the palace of the Sacred Serpent or Naga King, guardian of rivers. (56 cm high, 80 cm wide. Late 18th century).

115

Surrounded by grieving disciples, the dying Lord Buddha attains Parinirvana, release from the cycle of rebirths. A red robed monk appears between the curtains to comfort a follower. (73 cm high, 65 cm wide. Late 18th century).

Decorative Arts

In many societies the arts that embellish articles of ceremonial or daily use are relegated to second place, as mere 'crafts' or 'minor arts'. Yet these 'crafts' in some societies have been brought to a high point and reflect the great truths and preoccupations of that society. In Thailand the decorative arts that serve to ornament objects of daily and ceremonial use display a superb mastery of techniques as well as design.

There is a harmonious continuity in Thai design achieved through repetition and variation on themes. Many Thai designs are based on age long symbols: the lotus, the vegetation of the country, as well as 'imported' elements, mythologies and beliefs 'half as old as time', of divine guardians, celestial beings, demons, and creatures that are half-man (or woman) and half fabulous beast. These elements are harmoniously married and implemented in a variety of media: mother-of-pearl ware, lacquerware, silverware, nielloware and woodcarving to name but a few. Articles that may originate in humble usage, when made in precious metals or painstakingly decorated by skilled artisans go beyond the merely quotidian and become objects of delight, objects to be presented as offerings fit for divinities. Simple trays or dishes, suitably embellished, become ceremonial offering stands; mere doors or windows, suitably decorated, indicate passage from the everyday to royal or sacred areas. On a larger scale, the same themes are seen on majestic carved gableboards of monastery buildings and architectural decorations. Thus the decorative arts in Thailand reflect a harmonious conjunction of Hindu and Buddhist themes, originating long ago in India, but, over the centuries, thoroughly assimilated and reinterpreted in a uniquely Thai way. ■

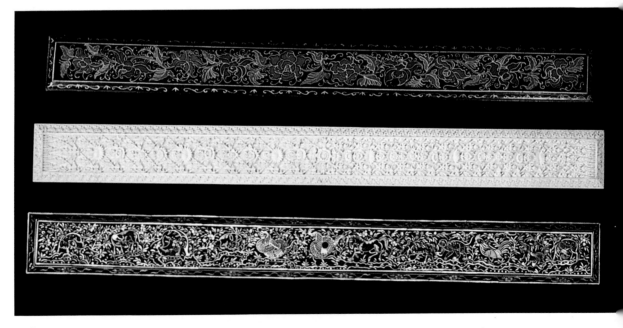

116

Scripture covers. Polychrome Lacquer, Ivory and Mother of Pearl. 60 cm long, 6 cm wide. Palm leaf scriptures were usually encased between such covers.

Mother – of – Pearl Inlay

The use of mother-of-pearl in inlaid decoration dates back as far as the sixth century A.D. in Thailand. Traces of it have been found in stucco embellishing a Dvaravati monument in the Ku Bua district in Ratchaburi province. Apart from one or two isolated fragments found on Buddha images from the Srivijaya (7th–14th century) and Chiang Saen (11th–14th century) periods, little is known of the evolution of this medium of decoration until its full flowering during the late Ayutthaya and early Bangkok periods (1757–1851) when it became popular to decorate doors, windows, furniture and vessels with mother-of-pearl inlay.

Thailand is noted for its distinctive *hoi fai* or flaming mother-of-pearl from the turbo snail indigenous to the Gulf of Thailand. This particular shell, on catching the light, emits a deep pink and green lustre reminiscent of fire opals, making other varieties of mother-of-pearl appear pale by comparison.

To decorate an object in mother-of-pearl requires infinite patience and meticulous attention to detail. An object has first to be made either of wood in the case of doors, shutters and bookcase panels, or of rattan in the case of circular vessels. The scene or design that is to decorate the object is sketched out in its entirety and is then transferred in the reverse onto tracing paper.

The shell, which is naturally curved, is cut with a small saw into pieces measuring approximately 2.5 cm. These pieces are then filed on a whetstone until they are reasonably flat. Since mother-of-pearl is brittle and tends to snap, these pieces are then glued to discs of wood which are twice the thickness of the shell. After reinforcing, the shell is then cut with a special curved bow saw to the desired shape. As cutting proceeds, each piece of shell is immediately pasted into place on the design tracing.

The object to be decorated with mother-of-pearl is given several separate coatings of lacquer—a resin from the yang or lacquer tree *(melanorrhoea usitata)*. While the final coat is still sticky, the mosaic of shell attached to the tracing paper is pressed face down into the lacquered surface. When the lacquer is completely dry, the tracing paper is peeled off by spraying with water. The hollows and ridges between the shell and lacquer surfaces are then filled with a paste made from pulverized

117

Detail of Table screen (see fig 119). A thepanom *celestial figure pays homage to Buddha's teachings from amidst foliage and Chinese style clouds.*

118

Phan waen fah *or two tiered recepta-cle. Mother-of-pearl inlay. 38.5 cm high. 19th century, Bangkok period. The up-per pedestalled vessel with sharp re-dented corners is decorated with a thepanom or praying celestial figure surrounded by branches and leaves of a flowering plant (khrua-bai-thet). It is set on a wide mouthed 12 sided stem-med tray called a* talum *which is em-bellished with a* bai thet *floral motif. This type of tiered vessel was formerly used for making presentations to a monastery.*

119

Table Screen. Mother-of-pearl inlay. 63.2 cm high, 45 cm wide. 19th century, Bangkok period. Panels such as this were placed upright on tables to serve as miniature screens. One of a pair, this screen depicts the Lord Buddha at the center of a flame decorated niche, at-tended by two of his favorite disciples, Mogellana and Sariputtra. Falling flow-ers behind them signify an auspicious event. Above, celestial beings look benignly down upon the scene.

74

charcoal mixed with lacquer. On modern work autobody filler may be used instead of lacquer. When completely dry, the lacquer surface is rubbed down with carborundum until it is completely smooth. Lastly the object is polished with a dried banana leaf impregnated with coconut oil.

The Museum has an outstanding collection of mother-of-pearl objects most of which date from the nineteenth century. The collection mainly consists of traditional round, polygonal and tiered vessels and containers which were once used in the homes of the wealthy, in court ceremonies and for conveying food and alms to monasteries.

One of the most well-known receptacles to be decorated with mother-of-pearl is the *talum*, a wide-mouthed container with sloping sides set on a high flaring pedestal, which was once used to carry alms such as flowers, incense and candles to a monastery. Thought to be of possible Khmer origin, the Museum has numerous hexagonal, octagonal and twelve-sided examples on display. Some may be seen in various sizes in sets of seven and eight. They may be piled high one on top of the other to resemble a stupa. Some *talum* support deep round bowls with sloping sides, called *khan nam* which were formerly used for storing lustral water.

The most striking of the food containers on display is the *tiep muk,* a wide bowl-like object supported on a small flaring foot ring and surmounted by a tall conical lid terminating in a knob. Ascribed to Khmer origin, this vessel was once used for either conveying offerings to monks or gifts to a bride at her wedding. Other food containers include the *lung,* a circular box which resembles a Chinese food container. This type of box was formerly used to store dry ingredients. The museum has some very good examples of *batra* or monks' begging bowls which are covered

120

Tiep muk *Mother-of-pearl inlay. 62 cm high, 49.5 cm diameter. 19th century, Bangkok period. This receptacle with a cone shaped cover was originally used to present alms or offerings to a monastery. The cover is decorated with* phum *or lotus bud shaped patterns surrounded by* kranok *or flame-like sprays.*

with round flat lids with sloping sides. Many of these *fa batra* covers are exquisitely decorated with mother-of-pearl in traditional designs. Some monks' bowls may be placed on a small flaring pedestal *cheng batra* which is also decorated with mother-of-pearl.

There are a number of small rectangular boxes which once served a variety of purposes. *Hiip buri* were used to store smoking materials, while medicines were kept in *hiip ya* boxes. Clothing presented by the King to nobles as insignia of rank was kept in a special box with sloping sides called a *jiad*. No collection of boxes in Thailand would be complete without a betel box. The Museum does have a number of these embellished with mother-of-pearl. The Museum has an extensive collection of trays, *kaba*, which, like boxes, served a number of religious and secular functions. Some are circular while others may be quadrilateral or octagonal with stepped corners. They are characterized by shallow straight sides and may either be set on moulded pedestals or supported by feet at the corners.

Mother-of-pearl was also considered a most worthy medium in which to decorate the highly revered manuscript or scripture boxes and wooden covers of religious books. The Museum has three types of manuscript boxes on display. Single manuscripts were generally stored in rectangular panelled boxes called *tuu nangsuu suat*, while a smaller portable box, the *hiip phra tham*, was used to keep copies of sermons and other loose papers. Monasteries usually stored religious manuscripts in tall cupboards with sloping sides called *tuu phra tham*.

121

Detail of the tiep muk depicted in fig. 120 showing a phum motif encircling a rajasingha *or royal lion motif.*

Musical instruments were also sometimes decorated with mother-of-pearl. The Museum has some outstanding examples of xylophones and small hand drums decorated in this medium.

The Museum mother-of-pearl collection is noteworthy for its depiction of traditional Thai ornamental motifs. The *krachang* or pointed leaf decoration, the trailing intertwining *kranok*, often terminating in fabulous ogres, snakes, bird's heads and animal masks, the lotus bud shaped *phum* and the *cho hang* rice ball designs may all be seen on examples of mother-of-pearl in the Museum collection. Hindu gods such as Vishnu astride his Garuda, Indra on his Erawan or three-headed elephant, graceful worshipping deva called *thepanom,* fierce ogres, lions, and birds, both real and imaginary, can also be seen cleverly integrated into the previously mentioned foliage designs. Religious episodes from the Life of the Buddha and scenes from the Ramayana may also be depicted in the mother-of-pearl medium. In addition to traditional ornamentation, Chinese influences can also be seen in naturalistic floral sprays and panoramic scenes which became popular during the reign of Rama III (1824–1851) ■

122

Batra or monk's bowl decorated with a cover and stand of mother-of-pearl. 21-8 cm diameter. The inlaid cover bearing the coat of arms of Rama V (1868-1910) depicts a triple-headed elephant or Erawan (detail above) flanked on the right by the rajasingha royal lion and on the left by the khotchasi or elephant lion. An inscription states that the vessel was made to be presented to the head of the Buddhist hierarchy in the year of the king's coronation. 1873.

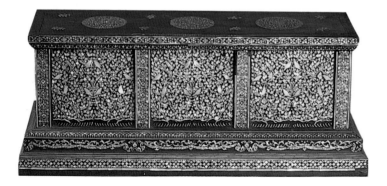

123

Tuu nangsuu suat manuscript chest. 33 cm high, 21 cm wide, 84 cm long. Bangkok period, 19th century. The panels are decorated with floral and bird designs.

124

Silverware

The center of silver craft traditions in Thailand is in Chiang Mai in the North. This region, known since 1296 as the Kingdom of Lan Na Thai, has a lengthy history as a cultural melting pot, and was incorporated into the Kingdom of Thailand as late as the reign of King Chulalongkorn, Rama V (1868–1910). Well prior to that, Burmese influence in the area was strong. Legend has it that in 1284, some five hundred families of silversmiths fled to the Chiang Mai region from Burma as refugees from the Mongol invasions.

Over succeeding centuries, such artisans became prizes of war, as the Burmese and the inhabitants of Lan Na struggled for supremacy in the region. Consequently, some cultural traditions, including that of silver-craft, are common to both countries, in which the art of the silver-smith has been a family concern for generations.

Until relatively recently, most Northern silver was derived from old coins of Indian, Indochinese and Chinese origin, attesting to overland trading between these regions since ancient times. These coins, some of which yield 92% silver, are melted down, and if necessary, alloyed with small percentages of copper, and then pounded into thin sheets. From these, objects of various shapes are made by fusing and appropriate pounding. Certain forms are popular both in the North and the rest of Thailand. Means of ornamentation include re-pousse, in which the raised relief pattern is achieved by hammering and working from the reverse or inside of the piece. This type of delicate workmanship requires the use of almost pure silver.

Many of the silver ceremonial wares in the National Museum collection were donated as gifts to the Museum. ∎

125

Ceremonial offering bowl and cover in the shape of a lotus, and detail of lotus finial above. Silver 50 cm high. Probably early 20th century. The bowl and cover feature exquisitely worked high relief lotus petals with a thepanom at the center of each. The lotus bud finial is decorated with the characteristic Thai flame or kranok design.

126

Water Flask, Silver. 38 cm high. Early 20th century. Decorated with floral patterns, this ornate flask replicates the shape of every day terracotla water flasks still in use in Thailand.

127

Offering stand. Silver. 20 cm high. Probably early 20th century. The upper section is formed by lotus leaf shaped designs inside of which alternate celestial or thepanom figures, and lion–like demon faces. Three sacred serpents or Nagas support the upper section.

128

Detail. Profile of sacred serpent support of extremely fine workmanship.

80

Nielloware

Exquisitely decorated ceremonial vessels of nielloware have long been popular in Thailand. It is thought that the art of nielloware may have been introduced here centuries ago by the Portuguese, and it seems that the still continuing tradition of presenting nielloware objects as State gifts dates back to the reign of King Narai of Ayutthaya (1656-1688). Nakhon Sri Thammarat in Southern Thailand has been the center of nielloware traditions for several centuries.

The process of decorating in niello is painstaking and complicated, requiring great skill from the craftsman. Briefly, the object to be decorated, usually of silver or gold is incised with a traditional Thai pattern. Those areas which are to be the background are carved in deep relief and filled with niello, a black composition consisting of metallic alloys of lead, copper and silver. The niello is fused with the metal of the object by heating. The object is then smoothed by hand with a file and polished. Extra details may also be incised during the filing and polishing process. In the finished product, the silver or gold base of the object stands out in shining contrast to the black matte background provided by the niello.

Thus objects, such as a humble teapot, when made from precious metals and decorated with painstaking skill, become luxury articles. to be admired and presented as gifts. ■

129

Cylinder and plungers for crushing betel nut. Gold Nielloware. 16 cm. 19th century, Bangkok period. In former times the ritual of betel nut chewing was widespread throughout Thai society. The quality of utensils associated with this custom reflected the rank of the owner.

130 ━━━━━━━━━

Tea Pot. Gold Nielloware. 15 cm high. 19th century, Bangkok Period. Underlying the deceptively simple overall floral design is an extraordinary degree of symmetrical balance. Gold nielloware objects were used exclusively by the Royal Household.

131 ━━━━━━━━━

Cylindrical lidded box. Gold Nielloware. 16 cm high. 19th century, Bangkok period. Chrysanthemum flowers and foliage in harmonious symmetry adorn this Royal utensil. Floral designs of Chinese derivation became popular in the early 19th century when trade with China was extensive.

Ivory Carving

Although long useful as a beast of burden in Southeast Asia, the elephant has been more valued for the precious ivory of its tusks, which have been turned into highly prized objects of ornamentation such as jewelry, knife handles, musical instruments, religious objects and even furniture. The nature of ivory lends itself well to the creation of intricate patterns which delight the eye, and an ivory carving is often more treasured than a similar piece worked in a precious metal. The delicacy of ivory carving became the supreme challenge to a master carver and as a consequence such artisans were held in high esteem.

To prepare ivory for carving, it must first be boiled in a solution to make it soft. It is then cut into the desired size pieces, the cutting going with the grain so as to prevent fracturing. The desired shape is outlined in charcoal, carved with delicate chisel strokes, smoothed with a file and finally polished to give it its characteristic gloss. Although ivory is durable, the humid climate of the tropics makes its preservation difficult. As a result ivory pieces found in Thailand are not very old.

Thai art is fundamentally religious: its purpose is to aid the viewer to achieve a mystical experience. Although objects of nature appear to figure in the design, the design itself is not meant to be a representation of the real world but rather a symbol of the spiritual world. For instance, plant life is a common theme found in Thai art. Plants grow and change and this is symbolic of the fundamental Buddhist precept that all things are in a state of continuous change. ∎

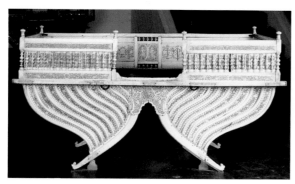

132, 133

Ivory Howdah (kub chang), above Height 90 cm, width 71 cm, length 174 cm. Detail, to right, back panel of seat, 14 cm high. This beautiful example of an intricately pierced design shows the ivory carvers' skill at its best. The howdah is a functional piece, a chair in effect, which because it is placed on the elephants back, must by definition be a sturdy piece of furniture. The grace and fluidity of the design gives the impression of lightness and delicacy which masks the actual size, weight and structural sturdiness of the piece. This howdah was presented to King Chulalongkorn by the Prince of Chiang Mai in the early 20th century.

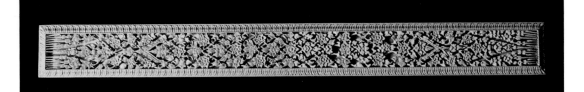

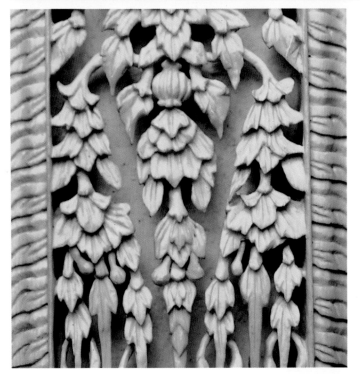

134, 135

Manuscript cover and detail. Ivory. 58 cm long, 5 cm wide. 19th century, Bangkok period.

Buddhist palm leaf manuscripts were placed between such covers. Intricately carved floral motif designs are repeated throughout the length of this ivory cover which terminates in fluted cone shaped floral designs and tendrils, reminiscent of present day flower garlands.

136, 137

Knife, and detail of handle. This ivory knife handle, of 10 cm length, depicts Hanuman, the monkey warrior of the Indian epic the Ramayana (the Ramakien in Thai) who is loved by the Thai for his bravery, quick wit and merry pranks. The detailed work in this carving is an exact replica of the costume and mask which would be worn by the human actor playing the role.

84

Lacquerware

Thailand is known as the leading exponent of the art of gold leaf decoration on lacquer in Southeast Asia. The raw material for lacquer decoration in Thailand is the sap of the *Melanorrhoea usitata,* **a tree native to Southeast Asia, which grows wild up to elevations of 3,000 feet. When tapped this tree emits a grey viscous liquid which turms to a glossy black on exposure to the air. The object to be decorated receives at least three successive coats of lacquer so that it acquires a lustrous smoothly polished surface.**

138

Tuu phra tham book cabinet. Black and gold lacquer, with sections of glass mosaic inlay. 218 cm high, 125 cm wide 17-18th century, Ayutthaya period. The door panels of this cabinet depict two foreign figures, possibly French and Persian, reflecting the presence of many such traders and diplomatic representatives in Ayutthaya, particularly during the reign of King Narai (1656–1688).

Using a pen or a brush with a very fine point, the craftsman carefully paints a freehand design with a water–soluble solution of gamboge – a yellow gummy resin. He paints only those parts of the design on which he wishes to retain the original black colour. The area to which gold is to adhere is left unpainted and is a negative of the design. A thin coat of lacquer or varnish is applied to those portions of the design which are to be covered with gold leaf. Tissue-thin squares of gold leaf are then pressed over the entire surface with a wad of cottonwool.

After drying in an underground cellar for twenty to twenty-four hours, but before the lacquer is absolutely hard, the entire object is washed with water to remove the excess gold leaf, varnish and yellow colouring matter. Thai lacquer work is referred to as *lai rod nam* which literally means ornaments washed with water. On contact with water the fully detailed gold leaf designs appear as if by magic against a glossy black background. The object is then returned to the cellar to harden.

Sometimes outlines of designs may be directly painted on to the surface of an object with gold paint. The background features such as trees and buildings may be highlighted with colour pigments, while the main figures are wrought in gold leaf using the *lai rod nam* technique.

Gilded lacquer decoration originated in China, but it is not yet known at what period and by what route this technique came to Thailand. The earliest extant examples of *lai rod nam* were made in the seventeenth century during the Ayutthaya period.

These early works are noted for their lively finely drawn animal and human figures set amidst traditional floral and vegetal *kranok* flame

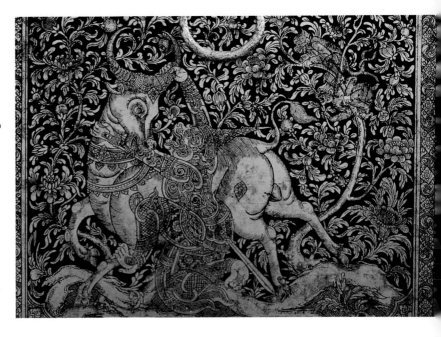

139

Detail of panel of chest. Black and gold lacquered wood. 53 cm high, 48 cm wide, 78 cm long. 17th century, Ayutthaya period. The decoration on this chest, considered to be one of the finest in existence, displays a harmonious balance between the gold details and the black background. Depicted here is the struggle between a realistically delineated buffalo and a stylised monkey. Surveying the scene from amidst naturalistic foliage and flowers is a pair of vividly realistic monkeys.

type decoration. These early works display a most subtle and harmonious balance between the gold leaf decoration and the black lacquer ground.

This style of decoration continued into the early Bangkok period (1782-1851). At the same time, panoramic–type pictures rendered in the style of a Thai painting began to become popular in *lai rod nam* work. These usually depict scenes from the Life of the Buddha and his previous existences, and the ever–popular Ramayana story.

During the Bangkok period, particularly during and after the reign of Rama III (1824–1851) Chinese influence gradually became more prevalent in gold leaf lacquer decoration. Gnarled trees with sinuous branches ending in sprigs of foliage amidst craggy twisted rocks provide a backdrop to scenes depicting traditional Thai figures. The blank empty spaces characteristic of Chinese work are occasionally relieved by flying butterflies and birds.

Although the gold leaf technique may be used to decorate a wide variety of everyday objects such as small boxes, vases and other vessels, the finest craftsmanship was usually reserved for objects intended for religious or royal use. The act of gilding in the Buddhist world is considered a meritorious deed and the best examples may be seen on window and door panels designed for palaces and wat compounds. The highly revered *tuu phra tham* book cabinets designed to store religious manuscripts were regarded as especially suitable objects on which to expend considerable effort and time on embellishment. Some of the best *lai rod nam* craftsmanship may be seen on storage boxes. Formerly, well-to-do people were known to store their clothes in large square boxes with flat or tiered lids which were often beautifully decorated with gold leaf designs. On the demise of the owner these boxes were often presented to monasteries to be used for the same purpose as the *tuu phra tham.*

The Museum has some excellent examples of lacquered clothes chests with tiered lids in the Red House (Tamnak Daeng) originally the home of Queen Sri Suriyen of King Rama II. These chests date back to the late Ayutthaya–early Bangkok periods. Fine examples of *tuu phra tham* manuscript chests may be seen in the Ayutthaya collection, in the minor arts of the Bangkok period section and in odd hallways of the former central Palace building. There are three fine examples of huge manuscript chests in the Buddhaisawan Chapel which depict scenes from the Ramayana story. These chests, commissioned by Rama III, were formerly used as room dividers in the Royal Palace.

Lacquered doors and windows with the vase of plenty designs may be seen in the Buddhaisawan Chapel. Chinese style gold leaf designs may be seen on the shutters of the Isarawinitchai Hall and on the inner buildings of the former central Palace. An opensided 'sala pavilion near the centre of the compound provides a good example of architectural highlighting in the gold leaf lacquer technique. ∎

140

Detail of screen. Black and gold lacquered wood. 145 cm high, 195 cm wide. (Actual screen is 175 cm wide, 255 cm high). Mid 19th century, Bangkok period. Housed in the Buddhaisawan Chapel, the screen depicts battle scenes from the Ramakien. In the lower section Lord Rama and the evil Tosakan are locked in combat on board a chariot surrounded by fighting monkeys and demons. Above them, opposing forces on chariots drawn by real and mythical animals prepare to do battle.

141

Detail of side panel of cabinet. Black and gold lacquered wood. 90 cm high, 70 cm wide. (Whole cabinet is 260 cm high. 420 cm long, 70 cm deep). The cabinet was commissioned in the mid 19th century by King Rama III. The detail shows a palace, at the center of which is depicted Hanuman the White Monkey in an encounter with a lady. It is characteristic of nineteenth century workmanship to deploy black and gold lacquer in the style of mural painting.

142

Detail from a door panel in the Wang Na Palace. Black and gold lacquer, restored 1982. Realistic birds and squirrels are depicted on a gnarled flowering tree. Compositions with a preponderance of black background suggest strong Chinese influence, popular since the mid 19th century.

143

Door panels in the Wang Na Palace. Black and gold lacquered wood. 290 cm high, 164 cm wide. Restored 1982. Topped by mythical monkeys in finely carved gilded foliage, these door panels reflect the fusion of Thai and Chinese designs. At the bottom are Thai mythical animals, variations of the singh or lion, while in the upper sections realistic creatures and birds frolic amid foliage and gnarled trees. The geometric panel at the center is characteristically Thai.

Woodcarving

Woodcarving is considered to be the most characteristically ' Thai ' of all the arts. It is thought to best illustrate the vitality and fertility of nature in both subject matter and technique. Wood was rarely used for Buddha images, but instead for furniture and the wide variety of fittings and ritual objects in the service of religion. Therefore, wood carvers were free of restrictive iconography. They often sought inspiration from their surroundings: the luxurious tropical vegetation and the real or imaginary creatures who populate it. This resulted in an emphasis on the decorative, on ornamentation, which is characteristic of Thai art. There is little concern for realism, for the human body, its movemment and drapery, all of which are of primary importance in Western art.

Unaffected by restrictions of material as experienced by bronze workers or stone sculptors, wood carvers employed a composite technique. This allowed an artist to carve the individual parts of a work separately and then assemble them. The resulting spontaneity parallels the creativity of nature.

Wood is an abundant material in most tropical countries and, as in India, may even have been worshipped in the form of tree spirits. Of the many varieties of wood available, teak is the material of choice because it is easy to carve, and relatively resistant to both termites and the elements.

The earliest remaining pieces date from the 16th century. Very few are found *in situ*, with the best preserved in museums. The highpoint of Thai woodcarving is found in images of lesser religious figures dating from the late Ayutthaya period (17th-early 18th century). The collection of the Bangkok National Museum features such fine pieces as the *kinnari*, half-bird half-human creatures, inhabitants of the Himaphan forest. The sophistication of these carvings suggests that there had been a rich developing tradition of woodworking over prior centuries, none of whose products survive.

Excellent workmanship continued into the early Bangkok period. The finest wood sculpture was closely associated with architecture, and animals were a favorite theme. ■

144

Kinnari 110cm high.
This masterpiece dates from the 17th or early 18th century. It represents a kinnari, a female half-human half-bird, living in one of the heavens high in the Himalayas. Its tail is in a stylized design called kranok, which is often found in Thai art. With its graceful movement and delicate, fine features and ornaments, it represents the best of the genre.

145

Carved and painted cabinet. Wood. 254 cm high. Teak library cupboards, this one dating from approximately 1750, were used to store palm-leaf manuscripts of Buddhist scriptures. They were just about the only items of furniture in a Buddhist wat, and ultimately derive their orgins from Chinese antecedents, as evidenced on this piece by the base of lion's claw feet with a dragon design between them.

This particular cabinet is an extraordinary piece, partly because it is one of only half a dozen surviving carved, as opposed to lacquered, cabinets. It is also unique in that its design of architectural elements is thought to represent an accurate picture of Ayutthaya shortly before its destruction in 1767

146

Detail of cabinet. The octagonal Chinese style building pictured at the bottom of the doors has been identified from 17th century European maps

147

Royal Funeral Chariot

The Vejayant Rajarot built by Rama I in 1785 is a royal funerary chariot used to transport the urn containing the body of the deceased from the wat to the crematorium. Made of teak, carved, gilded, and inlaid with glass, it is 40 feet high and weighs 40 tons. It is made of pegged parts which can be taken apart and reassembled. The tradition of using huge wooden chariots for gods and kings began in India. The Vejayant Rajarot is meant to symbolize Mt. Meru, the location of the heaven the deceased is about to enter. The forests of Mt. Meru are inhabited by mythological creatures who are represented on the chariot by nagas and devas, arranged in five tiers painted gold on top and red underneath. The tiers are separated by bands of inlaid colored glass. Altogether, the decoration appears as flames which reach up to engulf the urn placed on the top of the chariot under a canopy. Here the Vejayant Rajarot, renamed since the time of Rama VI as the great Chariot of Victory, is shown being returned to the National Museum after the funeral ceremonies for H.M. Queen Rambhai Bharni in 1985.

148

Detail of flame-like gilded lacquered carvings of sacred serpents or nagas on the Chariot.

Buddhaisawan Chapel, built in 1787 to enshrine the Phra Buddha Sihing image. Mural paintings depicting the Life of the Buddha line the interior walls.
Detail of Gable of Buddhaisawan Chapel.
The Samranmukkhamat Pavilion, an outstanding example of the Thai woodcarvers' art.

Gables and Chofa finials. This gable, the vertical triangular wall terminating a ridge roof structure, is from the Buddhaisawan Chapel in the grounds of the National Museum. Recently restored, the original dates from the end of the eighteenth century. Thai gables are carved in various designs, and often inlaid with colored glass. Hindu divinities frequently appear on Thai Buddhist architecture. This gable depicts the four-faced, four armed Hindu god Brahma in a central celestial pavilion, flanked by smaller pavilions also enshrining Brahma. From the background foliage emerge more manifestations of Brahma. All figures have hands clasped at the breast, the position of paying homage to the Buddhist teachings enshrined in the Chapel below.

Traditional Thai decorative elements are abundant, below, on the Samranmukkhamak Pavilion or 'sala.' Celestial beings and carved foliage based on variations of lotus and kranok flame designs contribute to the masterly effect.

The chofa or finial literally means a bunch of sky' or ' sky tassel.' These finials are found on royal and religious buildings only, and may vary from region to region. They are thought to represent a Hamsa or celestial goose that the god Brahma rides, or the Garuda, the vehicle of the Hindu god Vishnu. Such architectural elements serve no functional purpose but reflect religious symbolism. An oft repeated motif is the Naga, a semidivine being usually in serpent form, king of the terrestial waters and a protector of Buddhism. On the gableboard, of the Samranmukkhamat Pavilion, the body of the Naga or sacred serpent undulates from the apex and culminates in multiple flaring heads at both outer edges of the roof eaves.

Masks

In many Southeast Asian countries, theatrical performances — puppet or human — are closely associated with ritual. In Thailand, vestige of this once religious connection remains in the *wai khru* ceremony of saluting esteemed teachers before a performance.

Episodes from the *Ramakien*, the Thai adaptation of the Indian *Ramayana* epic, are popular, and are performed by masked actors and dancers miming to words narrated or sung off stage, to the accompaniment of the *piphat* percussion orchestra. This type of performance is known as the *khon* or masked drama. Although formerly all performers wore masks, nowadays only demon and animal characters wear them. Each mask has special features and colors which clearly identify individual characters to the audience.

152

Mask of Hanuman. The well-known white monkey warrior of Phra Ram's army was assigned to search for Nang Sida (Sita), the abducted wife of Phra Ram. This splendid example shows Thai mask making at its finest. The basic foundation is of papier maché overlain with small pieces of mother-of-pearl which is designed to depict the character of Hanuman, often described as having "diamond hair and crystal fangs" size H 25 cm

153 ▪ 154

Mask of Phra Ram (Rama). The Supreme Commander of the Pavilion army wears a tall, pointed crown which imitates the shape of Thai temple spires. In Thai drama the mask for Rama is painted green. Rama's features — almond eyes, gentle smile, thin lips — are delicate and fit with his refined movements and calm, carefully controlled speech Height 68 cm.

Mask of Tosakan (Ravana). This Supreme Commander of the demon army of Langka has identical demonic faces arranged on the crown and a celestial face at the top to show his descent from a god.

Tosakan, the arch enemy of Rama, has eyes that are rounded and bulge, his teeth protrude and his nose is prominent. Height 67 cm.

Marionettes

Theatrical performances using shadow puppets have long been popular, particularly in Southern Thailand. In recent times, there has been a general revival of interest in performances using rod puppets, as well as string operated marionettes.

Three dimensional puppets or marionettes are known by the term *hun*. Of particular note in the National Museum collection are the recently restored Hun Luang, or Royal Puppets. These puppets appear unique to Thailand in that they were manipulated from below by a complex set of strings enabling the arms, hands and fingers to curve and bend in imitation of the graceful movements of the human dancer. Hun Thai or Hun Lek was smaller in size than the Hun Luang and had fewer strings for manipulation.

155
Hun Lek puppet. Hanuman. As the leader of the simian army which comes to the aid of Lord Rama in his battles against the evil Tosakan. Hanuman is identifiable by his white mask and small coronet. Heigh 25 cm.

156 - 157
Hun Luang Puppets. 42 cm high. Late 19th century, restored 1986. To left, Leading Demon Character, Phra Pirap. To right, Leading Male Character, Phra Prot. When manipulated by the numerous strings from below, these puppets may perform intricate stylised gestures.

GLOSSARY

Amitabha : 'The Buddha of Infinite Light' in Mahayana (q.v.) and Vajrayana Buddhism (q.v.) who lives in the Western Paradise, the 'Pure Land' By calling upon him, one can be reborn in his paradise and thus ensure the attainment of Buddhahood in one's next rebirth. Avalokitesvara. (q.v.)

Apsaras : Celestial nymphs who sing and dance for the pleasure of gods and fallen heroes.

Avalokitesvara : The 'Lord who looks down with compassion', the most popular bodhisattva (q.v.) in Mahayana Buddhism (q.v.). He is an emanation of the Amitabha Buddha (q.v.) and wears an image of the latter in his headdress. Also appears in the form of Padmapani (q.v.).

Avatar : The descent of a deity from heaven to earth. The term usually refers to one of the ten reincarnations on earth of the god Vishnu.

Bencharong : This term, meaning ''five colors'' was applied to a type of enamelled porcelain originally made in China to Thai specifications.

Bodhisattva : In Mahayana Buddhism (q.v.), a being who has achieved enlightenment but renounces Buddhahood until all beings reach the same goal by the saving power of his compassion. In both Theravada (q.v.) and Mahayana Buddhism (q.v.), the term is also applied to the earlier lives of the historical Buddha as well as to Gautama (q.v.) prior to his enlightenment.

Bodhi Tree : The sacred tree *(ficus religiosa)* under which Gautama meditated and achieved enlightenment, becoming henceforth known as the Buddha. In early Buddhist Art, aniconic symbols such as the Bodhi Tree were used to indicate the presence of the Buddha in a scene.

Brahma : The creator in the Hindu trinity (Vishnu is the preserver, and Shiva the destroyer). Frequently depicted with 4 faces and 4 arms, he appears in Buddhist Art, along with Indra, as an attendant of the Buddha.

Buddha : An enlightened being who has achieved a perfect understanding of the causes of human suffering and the means whereby to overcome them, thereby being freed from all further rebirth. In Theravada Buddhism the term is restricted to the historic Buddha who lived in the 6th c. B.C. (Siddhartha Gautama), and to a series of Buddhas who appeared on earth in previous eras (but did not preach the doctrine), or Maitreya, the Buddha of the future (q.v.).

Chakra : Wheel, disc, symbol of the sun, attribute of the god Vishnu. In Buddhism, the Wheel is the symbol of the doctrine which the Buddha set into motion when he preached the first Sermon.

Chakri : The dynasty that has reigned in Thailand since 1782.

Chedi : In Thailand it is used to signify a solid religious monument built to enshrine the relics of the Buddha or holy men, and also to contain the ashes of the dead. The words *chedi* and *stupa* (q.v.) are often interchangeable.

Deva : (male), **Devi :** (female) A celestial being who lives in one of the six lower heavens of Buddhist cosmology.

Ekamukhalinga : Phallic symbol of the god Shiva adorned with the god's face carved in relief.

Erawan : The three–headed elephant, vehicle of the god Indra.

Garuda : A mythical bird, king of the birds and natural enemy of the nagas (q.v.). It has a human body but the wings, legs and beak of a bird. It is the vehicle of the god Vishnu.

Gautama : The clan name of the historic Buddha who was called *Siddhartha* as a prince; *Gautama* when he became an ascetic; and the *Buddha* after he achieved Enlightenment.

Himaphan : A mythical forest in Buddhist cosmology located in the Himalayas below the heavens of the gods, inhabited by both real and imaginary animals.

Hinayana : 'Lesser Way' or 'Lesser Means of Progression' a derogatory term used by Mahayana (q.v.) Buddhists in referring to the non-Mahayana sect, especially the Theravada (q.v.) which claims to be closer to the original teachings of the Buddha.

Jataka : 'Birth Story', referring to the 547 tales of the previous lives of the Buddha. In Thailand, the 10 lives preceding the Buddha's birth as Prince Siddhartha Gautama are most popular, and are frequently depicted in mural paintings. Each story represents a virtue practised to perfection.

Kinnara : (male), **Kinnari :** (female) A divine musician, half-human and half-bird in form who lives in the Himaphan forest.

Kranok : A flame-like design popular in the decorative elements of Thai Art.

Mahayana Buddhism : 'Greater Way' or 'Greater Means of Progression', a major branch of Buddhism emerging in Northern India at the beginning of the Christian era and attaching essential importance to speculations on the nature of the Buddhas and to the role of the bodhisattvas (q.v.). It is often called Northern Buddhism because it is chiefly practised in Nepal, Tibet, China, Korea, Japan and Vietnam.

Maitreya : In both Theravada (q.v.) and Mahayana Buddhism (q.v.) the Buddha of the future, who is at present a bodhisattva (q.v) dwelling in Tusita heaven. In sculpture, he is depicted with a stupa in his headdress.

Mara : Personified evil, sensual pleasure and delusion, tempter of the Buddha. At Enlightenment the Buddha achieved Victory over Mara and all that Mara represents.

Meru : also Sumeru : A mythical mountain, the centre of the Universe around which the continents and oceans are placed. Located on Mt. Meru is Tavatimsa heaven (q.v.) ruled by Indra.

Muchalinda : King of the nagas (q.v.) who protects the meditating Buddha during a storm shortly after his Enlightenment by surrounding him with his coils and sheltering him with his multi-headed hood.

Mudra : The ritual gesture of the hands, each gesture indicating a specific action or power. In Theravada Buddhist art, the principal *mudras* are as follows:

Abhaya mudra : gesture of reassurance or Dispelling Fear.

Bhumisparsa mudra or *Maravijaya mudra :* gesture of Victory over Mara or Calling the Earth to Witness.

Dharmachakra mudra : gesture of Preaching the First Sermon or Setting the Wheel of Law in Motion.

Dhyana mudra : gesture of Meditation.

Vara mudra : gesture of charity or Bestowing Favours.

Vitarka mudra : gesture of Teaching. In Thailand, this gesture executed with both hands, is called *Descending from Tavatimsa Heaven*.

Naga : A snake or serpentine divinity that dwells in the subterranean and water regions. Nagas guard the hidden treasures of the earth and control rainfalls. They are the arch enemies of the garudas (q.v.). The struggle between the two is a frequent theme in art.

Nirvana : 'Extinction' or 'blowing out', the state of release from earthly bonds, suffering and delusion, and thus liberation from the cycle of rebirths. It is the condition one attains upon enlightenment while still living on earth; the Buddha reached *nirvana* under the bodhi tree. *Parinirvana* is the perfect or complete *nirvana* attained at the time of death.

Padmapani : 'He who holds the lotus', another form of the bodhisattva Avalokitesvara. The lotus symbolises his creative powers.

Stupa : Originally meaning a burial mound for princes in ancient India. It very early became the most important type of Buddhist monument enshrining the relics of the Buddha, of his disciples or to mark an important site in Buddhism. A *stupa* is basically a solid monument consisting of a dome (of variable shape) supported by a base and surmounted by a tiered umbrella with differing degrees of stylization. In Thailand it has the same meaning as the word *chedi* (q.v.).

Tantric Buddhism : An advanced stage of Vajrayana Buddhism (q.v.), important in Northeast India after the 8th c. and surviving in Nepal and Tibet. It flourished briefly in the Khmer empire in ancient times. This school tremendously expanded the Buddhist pantheon including the creation of fearsome multi-limbed, multi-headed deities. Emphasis is placed on esoteric worship practices to enable a devotee to effect union with his god through visual images, symbols, repetition of sounds, prescribed movements and breath control. Worship of the female energy of the god is also important.

Tavatimsa Heaven : Heaven of the thirty-three gods on top of Mount Meru (q.v.) over which Indra presides.

Thepanom : The figure of a deva or devi (q.v.) with hands in a worshipping gesture; a celestial being.

Theravada Buddhism : 'The School or Teaching of the Elders', it is today the only surviving school of early Buddhism. Its teaching is preserved in the Pali Canon and is used by the Buddhists of Sri Lanka, Burma, Thailand, Cambodia and Laos. Also known as Southern Buddhism. Often called Hinayana, the rather derogatory term which means 'the Lesser Way', as opposed to Mahayana, 'the Greater Way.' This sect emphasises individual effort towards Enlightenment, whereas the Mahayana abounds with bodhisattvas, or saint-like beings to whom devotees may pray for help along the way to understanding. *(see Mahayana and Hinayana Buddhism)*.

Vajrayana Buddhism : 'The Way of the Thunderbolt' or 'the Diamond Vehicle', a development in Mahayana Buddhism (q.v.) which began in Northeast India about the 4th c. A.D. and reached its full development by the 8th c. A.D. From India, especially in its advanced Tantric form (q.v.), it moved to Nepal, Tibet and China. *Vajrayana* stresses worship practices that enable the devotee to attain union with the Great Universal Spirit through the use of mystical incantation, formulas, magical diagrams, ritual gestures and yoga.

Further Reading :

Boisselier, Jean. **The Heritage of Thai Sculpture.** Weatherhill, New York and Tokyo, 1975.

Boisselier, Jean. **Thai Painting.** Kodansha International,Tokyo, New York and San Francisco, 1976.

Brown, Roxanna. **The Ceramics of South-East Asia : Their Dating and Identification.** Oxford University Press, Kuala Lumpur, London, New York, 1977.

Cadet, J.M. **The Ramakien.** Kodansha International, Tokyo and Palo Alto, 1971.

Charoenwongsa, Pisit, and Diskul, Subhadradis, M.C. **Thailand : Archaeologia Mundi Series.** Nagel Publishers, Geneva, Paris, Munich, 1978.

Chongkol, Chira. **Guide to the National Museum Bangkok.** Department of Fine Arts, Bangkok, 1986.

Coedes, G. **The Indianised States of Southeast Asia.** East-West Center Press, University of Hawaii, 1968.

Diskul, Subhadradis, M.C. **Art in Thailand : A Brief History.** Silpakorn University, Bangkok, 1986.

Diskul, Subhadradis, M.C. (ed). **The Art of Srivijaya.** UNESCO, Paris, 1980.

Diskul, Subhadradis, M.C. et al. **The Suan Pakkad Palace Collection.** Aksorn Samphan Press, Bangkok, 1982.

Diskul, Subhadradis, M.C. and Rice, Charles. **The Ramakien (Ramayana) Mural Paintings along the Galleries of the Temple of the Emerald Buddha.** Government Lottery Office, Bangkok, 1981.

Fickle, Dorothy. **The Life of the Buddha : Murals in the Buddhaisawan Chapel. National Museum Bangkok.** Fine Arts Department 1979.

Fickle, Dorothy. **A Glossary of Terms Used in the Arts of Thailand.** National Museum Volunteers, Bangkok, 1974.

Krairiksh, Piriya. **Art Styles in Thailand : A Selection from National Provincial Museums.** Fine Arts Department, Bangkok, 1977.

Krairiksh, Piriya. **Art in Peninsular Thailand Prior to the 14th Century A.D.** Department of Fine Arts, Bangkok, 1980.

Krairiksh, Piriya. **The Sacred Image : Sculptures from Thailand.** Catalogue for An Exhibition organised by the Museum for East-Asian Art of the City of Cologne in Collaboration with the Department of Fine Arts and the National Museum, Bangkok, 1979.

Rajavaramuni, Phra. **Thai Buddhism in the Buddhist World.** Maha Chulalongkorn Alumni Association, Maha Chulalongkorn Buddhist University, Wat Mahathat, Bangkok, 1985.

Robinson, Natalie V. **Sino-Thai Ceramics in the National Museum, Bangkok, Thailand, and in Private Collections.** Department of Fine Arts, Bangkok, 1982.

Rooney, Dawn F. **Khmer Ceramics.** Oxford University Press., Singapore, Oxford, New York, 1984.

Sawaddi Magazine and National Museum Volunteers Bangkok. **The Artistic Heritage of Thailand : A Collection of Essays.** Bangkok, 1979.

Shaw, J.C. **Northern Thai Ceramics.** Oxford University Press Kuala Lumpur, 1981.

Spinks, Charles Nelson. **The Ceramic Wares of Siam.** 3rd revised ed. The Siam Society, Bangkok, 1978.

Stratton, Carol, and Scott, Miriam McNair. **The Art of Sukhothai : Thailand's Golden Age.** Kuala Lumpur, Oxford University Pres 1981.

White, Joyce C. **Ban Chiang : Discovery of a Lost Bronze Age.** Catalogue for an exhibition organised by The University Museum, University of Pennsylvania; The Smithsonian Institution Travelling Exhibition Service; The National Museums Division, Department of Fine Arts, Thailand, 1982.

Wray, Elizabeth et al. **The Ten Lives of the Buddha.** Siamese Temple Paintings and Jataka Tales. Weatherhill, New York and Tokyo, 1974.

CONTRIBUTORS

The National Museum Volunteers offer their sincere thanks to the following past and present Steering Committee members, without whose advice, inspiration and leadership this publication would not have been possible:

Former Research Group Chairman * Martine Dean *
Former Thai Art and Culture Tour Leader * Kay de Groot *

Former Coordinators * Doris Schulz de Sepulveda
  * Paulette de Schaller * Virginia M.Di Crocco *
  * Rita Ringis * Fumiko Boughey * Janine Gray *
Present Coordinator * Mira Kim Prachabarn *

Photography

Pam Taylor National Museum Volunteers Photographer

1-3 • 23 • 35 • 38 • 41 • 44 • 48 • 69 • 75 • 77 • 78 • 81 • 84 – 131 • 133 – 156 •

Somchai Vorasastra National Museum Staff Photographer

4–22 • 24 – 34 • 36 • 37 • 39 • 40 • 42 • 43 • 45 – 47 • 49 – 68 • 70 – 74 • 76 • 79 • 80 • 82 • 83 • 132 •

CONTRIBUTORS

Coordinating Editor Rita Ringis
Layout Editor Helene Sackstein
Layout Staff Martine Dean * Rita Ringis * Heilan Renshaw *
Philaivan Sindusopon * Cathy Lacoste *
Rosemary Whitcraft * Betsy Harmon *

Writers

James V. Di Crocco	*Prehistory*
Sarah McLean	*Sculpture*
Eileen Deeley	*Mon Dvaravati Sculpture*
Rita Ringis	*Ancient Hindu Gods Sculpture*
Paulette de Schaller	*Srivijaya and Peninsular Sculpture*
Virginia M. Di Crocco	*Khmer and Lopburi Sculpture*
Mira Kim Prachabarn	*Lan Na Thai Sculpture*
Rita Ringis	*Sukhothai Sculpture*
Janine Gray	*U Thong Sculpture*
Janine Gray	*Ayutthaya Sculpture*
Ruth Gerson	*Ratanakosin Sculpture*
Dr. Dawn Rooney	*Ceramics*
Rita Ringis	*Mural Painting*
Sylvia Fraser–Lu	*Mother–of–Pearl Inlay*
Danielle Wiedmann	*Silverware*
Danielle Wiedmann	*Nielloware*
Ann Parsons	*Ivory Carving*
Sylvia Fraser–Lu	*Lacquerware*
Ardis Willwerth	*Woodcarving*
Ann Parsons	*Masks and Marionettes*
Eileen Deeley	*Glossary*

Editing and Proof Reading Rita Ringis * James V.Di Crocco * Heilan Renshaw *
Janine Gray * Barbara Montgomery * Carolyn Young *
* Winnie Durongpadiya * Melanie Pomfret *

Special Thanks are also due to the following members for their assistance :
Linda Bigelow * Margot Bittenbender * Penelope Clapp * Vonnie Franda *
Gaye Paterson Lamb * Judy Pauker * Barbara Rowbottom * Marisa Sekles *
* Srikasame Kasemsri * Maria Whiteley * Gage Wilks *

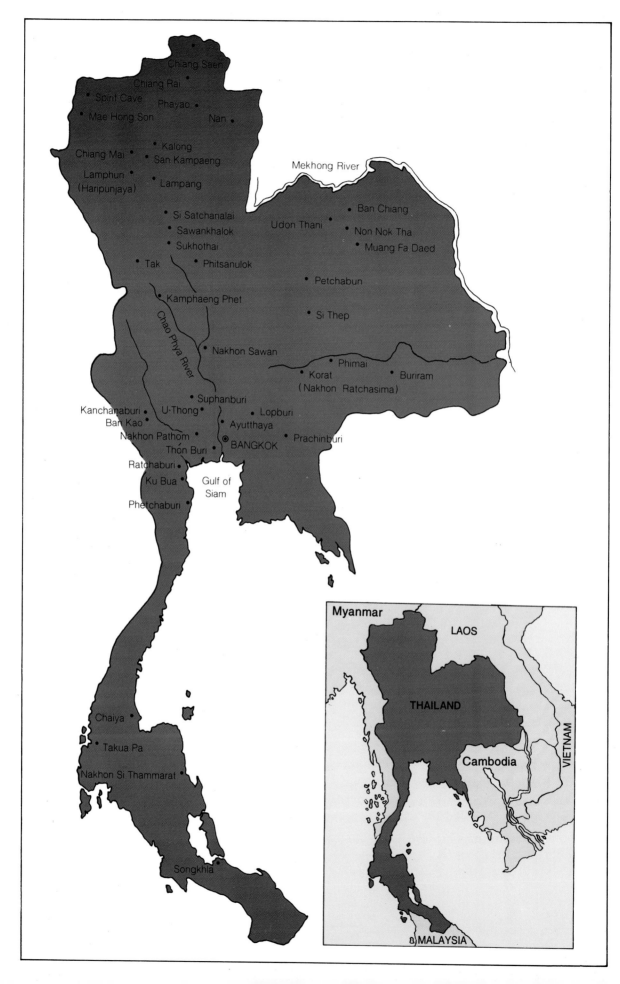

Chiang Saen

Chiang Rai

Spirit Cave

Phayao

Mae Hong Son

Nan

Kalong

Chiang Mai

San Kampaeng

Lamphun
(Haripunjaya)

Lampang

Mekhong River

Si Satchanalai

Udon Thani

Ban Chiang

Sawankhalok

Non Nok Tha

Sukhothai

Muang Fa Daed

Tak

Phitsanulok

Petchabun

Kamphaeng Phet

Si Thep

Chao Phya River

Nakhon Sawan

Phimai

Korat
(Nakhon Ratchasima)

Buriram

Suphanburi

Kanchanaburi

U-Thong

Lopburi

Ban Kao

Ayutthaya

Nakhon Pathom

Prachinburi

Thon Buri

BANGKOK

Ratchaburi

Ku Bua

Gulf of
Siam

Phetchaburi

Chaiya

Takua Pa

Nakhon Si Thammarat

Songkhla

Myanmar

LAOS

THAILAND

VIETNAM

Cambodia

MALAYSIA